REMEMBER THE 70s

This edition first published in the UK in 2006
by Green Umbrella Publishing

Printed and bound in Italy

ISBN: 1-905009-65-8
ISBN-13: 978-1-905009-65-7

REMEMBER THE 70s

Edited by Michael Heatley

Written by Alan Kinsman, Chris Mason, Ian Welch and Claire Welch

1970 1971 1972 1973 1974 1975 1976 1977 1978 1979

CONTENTS

REMEMBER THE SEVENTIES

1970

FASHION, CULTURE & ENTERTAINMENT

Monty Python

The BBC satirical comedy *Monty Python's Flying Circus* was a huge hit of 1970. Starring Graham Chapman, John Cleese, Terry Gilliam, Eric Idle, Terry Jones and Michael Palin, the sketches were centred on some of the most explosive issues of the time including sex, racism, politics, drugs, mice and molluscs to name but a few. But, the outstanding writing ability from members of the cast turned the show into a huge hit which quickly gained a cult following. With weird and imaginative animation from Terry Gilliam binding sketches, the show sparkled with innovative ideas and pushed the boundaries of acceptability in terms of both style and content. The group chose the name Monty Python purely because they thought it sounded funny.

Cleese and Chapman first met at Cambridge University where they were joined a year later by Idle – all three were members of Footlights – while Palin and Jones met at Oxford University. While on tour with Footlights, Cleese met Gilliam in New York. The Pythons were first united in *The Frost Report*, a satirical television programme hosted by Sir David Frost (who was secretary of Footlights when Cleese, Chapman and Idle were members).

Sketches relied on off-beat domestic situations and spoof TV interviews or documentaries, where often scenes were ended half way through. With bad taste and incomprehensibility it shocked and confused but was undoubtedly inspired. Juvenile pranks and general silliness were rife, particularly in

skits such as *The Dead Parrot* where John Cleese confronts Palin, playing a shopkeeper, with a dead bird he'd just purchased and 'The Lumberjack Song' which begins as a rousing chorus of machismo but

Above: Portrait of Monty Python (left to right) John Cleese, Graham Chapman, Michael Palin, Terry Jones, and Eric Idle.
Below: The pyramid stage at the second Glastonbury Festival.

1970 1971 1972 1973 1974 1975 1976 1977 1978 1979

Festival and was inspired by Eavis attending an open-air concert by Led Zeppelin at the Bath and West Showground earlier that same year. Today, Glastonbury is the largest greenfield music and performing arts festival in the world, best known for its contemporary music, dance, comedy, theatre, circus and cabaret.

The festival in 2005 attracted more than 150,000 people and had over 385 live performances. Initially, Glastonbury (as it became known in 1971) was heavily influenced by hippie ethics and the free festival movement and is still held today at Worthy Farm, six miles west of Glastonbury itself, overlooking Glastonbury Tor in the vale of Avalon. Many of the earlier festival ideals including Green Futures healing and alternative culture, still exist today.

The second festival held in 1971 called Glastonbury Fayre (filmed by David Puttnam and Nicolas Roeg) was influenced by Andrew Kerr and Arabella Churchill (granddaughter of Winston) and saw the use of the first

quickly turns into a celebration of transvestism.

Monty Python wasn't just confined to television and led to stage shows, four films, books, albums and computer games.

Glastonbury

The Glastonbury Festival for Contemporary Performing Arts was first held for 1,500 people in 1970. Created by Michael Eavis, the small-scale event was initially called the Pilton

Below: The summer solstice celebrations at the Glastonbury Festival.

pyramid stage. Erected from scaffolding and metal sheeting, it was paid for by voluntary contribution and the medieval tradition of music, dance, poetry, theatre and spontaneous entertainment re-emerged therein as jazz and folk music.

The festival lapsed until an unplanned event in 1978 which was followed by an unsuccessful festival the following year. Since 1981, however, Glastonbury has gone from strength to strength despite several years when the festival has not taken place. Apart from technical and security staff the festival is run by volunteers while Oxfam organises stewards. Volunteer staff are recruited from small charities and campaign groups who are rewarded for their work with free entry to the festival, food, transport and donations to their charities by the organisers.

The Goodies

The Goodies ran from November 1970 to February 1982 and was a surreal television series combining sketches and situation comedy. Created, written and starring Graeme Garden, Tim Brooke-Taylor and Bill Oddie, the show comprises the trio taking on bizarre assignments such as guarding the Crown Jewels, rescuing London from a giant kitten and attempting to put their own world improvement schemes into action.

Above: From left to right, Bill Oddie, Tim Brooke-Taylor and Graeme Garden, stars of 'The Goodies'.

Although they have common goals, each plays a very different part: Brooke-Taylor is weedy and a royalist; Garden is a mad scientist; while Oddie is an unkempt socialist and cynic. Their plots were bound together by slapstick sketches and spoof commercials.

As well as enjoying TV success, the Goodies also produced successful books such as *The Goodies File* and The *Goodies Book Of Criminal Records* as well as chart singles including 'The Funky Gibbon' and 'The Inbetweenies'.

Skirt wars – the mini, the midi and the maxi

In 1970, women had choice. No longer confined to either the miniskirt or trousers, the trendy midiskirt and maxidress were now available. It was imperative to make a fashion statement by the 1970s – for some the chunkier the better for others soft and feminine the preferred choice.

Fashions were outrageous and the miniskirt virtually disappeared (to the disappointment of many men) in favour of the longer length skirts. The midi length came below the knee while the maxi reached floor-level. Evening wear became liberated and women often chose to wear a floor-length maxidress with typical straight or flared empire lines, often with a sequinned fabric bodice and exotic sleeves. In contrast to the mini which tended to reveal all, women opted for longer lengths claiming that the miniskirt exploited women rather than liberated them.

Stylophone

In 1967, Dubreq was founded by Brian Jarvis, his brother Ted Jarvis and Burt Coleman.

Together, they worked in the broadcasting and film industry, dubbing and recording film soundtracks – hence the company name, Dubreq.

Brian Jarvis invented the stylophone which was to become a runaway success in 1970 when the company brought in Rolf Harris and his jolly personality to promote the product. Consisting of a metal keyboard that was played by touching the keys with a stylus, the miniature electronic musical instrument was more of a toy and gimmick than a serious musical instrument. Each note was connected to a cheap voltage-controlled oscillator via a different value resistor which, when touched by the stylus, closed the circuit and created a

Below: Fashion in 1970.

note. More than three million stylophones were sold, mostly to children.

Despite its gimmick status, David Bowie used a few notes on a stylophone on his hit 'Space Oddity' and German group Kraftwerk, known for their promotion of electronic music, used it extensively on their album 'Computer World'. It also featured on Orbital's 1999 single 'Style'.

MUSIC

March

Having worked solidly with backing outfit the Grease Band ever since his '68 Number 1 'With A Little Help From My Friends', singing gas-fitter Joe Cocker flew into Los Angeles for some much-needed rest and

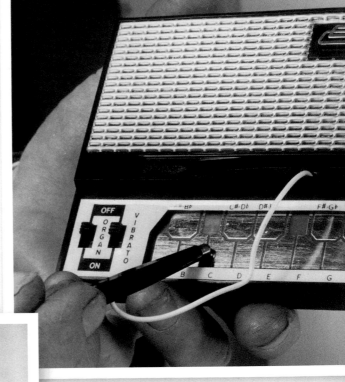

recuperation – only to find himself facing a tour of 58 nights in 48 US cities! Cancelling would, it was heavily hinted, impair his chances of ever working in the States again. Enter Oklahoman keyboard-player Leon Russell, who assembled an 11-piece band and 10-piece backing 'choir' in just four frantic days to help a frazzled Cocker fulfil his commitments.

The Mad Dogs and Englishmen Tour left Joe 'in a heap in Los Angeles', down and disillusioned with music and all that went with it. Peter Green-style tales of discarded, uncashed royalty cheques – not to mention some undesirable rock'n'roll habits picked up on the road – suggested he'd turned his back for good. But fortunately Cocker survived to sing

Above: The infamous Stylophone!
Below: Joe Cocker in action.

again, and remains a classic rocker today.

April

Review copies of Paul McCartney's debut solo album were sent out during the second week of the month, each including a question and answer 'interview', written by McCartney, which broke the news to the world that the Beatles were no more. Ironically, McCartney was the last of the Beatles to fly the coop – Ringo Starr had left briefly during the turbulent sessions for the White Album in 1968, George Harrison had walked out during the filming of *Let It Be* the following January, and in September 1969 John Lennon had 'wanted a divorce' following the completion of 'Abbey Road' – but in each case their disagreements were kept quiet, and the world remained blissfully unaware.

The dream, however, was well and truly over. After the disastrous *Let It Be* project, the Beatles had regrouped briefly to produce 'Abbey Road', regarded by many as one of their finest achievements. The album's final recording session, on 20 August 1969, marked the last time all four Beatles would be in a studio together, and by the end of the year Lennon was busy with the Plastic Ono Band and numerous media projects with wife Yoko Ono, and Starr had started work on what would become his debut solo album, 'Sentimental Journey'. McCartney completed his first solo offering during the spring, recording both at home and at Morgan Studios in north-west London, where he booked sessions under the pseudonym Billy Martin. The project was shrouded in secrecy, and not even the other Beatles were aware of what was happening, in retrospect an indication of how far relations had deteriorated between the Fab Four.

Lennon, especially, was angry that McCartney had stolen his thunder, and the announcement began

Below: Paul and Linda McCartney on their farm, the day after McCartney started High Court proceedings to seal the final break-up of the Beatles.

1970 1971 1972 1973 1974 1975 1976 1977 1978 1979

several years of infighting and bitterness between the former partners, all made worse by the countless lawsuits surrounding the group's affairs that dragged on throughout the first half of the decade.

August

The third, and until 2002, final Isle of Wight Festival took place over five days at the end of August 1970, featuring many of the biggest names of the day. The festival became regarded as Britain's 'Woodstock', and remains the biggest music festival ever held in the UK. An estimated 600,000 people crammed onto Afton Down to see such legendary performers as Jimi Hendrix, the Doors, Miles Davis and The Who.

But the festival proved to be a logistical nightmare, and became the focus for anti-capitalist and anarchist groups who objected to the £3 admission charge and encouraged fans to break into the site for free. Many did, destroying the perimeter fence and causing havoc for police and festival organisers. Years later, this conflict between the hippie idealism of the 1960s and the commercial imperative of the 1970s was graphically illustrated in Murray Lerner's film of the event, *Message To Love*.

In truth, some of the performers were not at their best, most notably the Doors and, disappointingly, Jimi Hendrix. Hendrix suffered technical problems during the early part of his set, and his subsequent efforts could best be described as erratic, a crying shame given that this proved to be the last major show

he would play. There were, however, some notable triumphs, with barnstorming sets from home-grown acts like Family, the Who and Jethro Tull to keep the fans happy, and a characteristically eccentric performance from the surprise hit of the event, Tiny Tim. Outside the main arena, perennial festival favourites Hawkwind and the Pink Fairies did their thing in a large tent that became known as 'Canvas City', presaging the multi-stage approach of later similar events at Glastonbury and elsewhere.

Immediately after the event, though, promoter Ron Foulk was adamant – 'This is the last festival – it

Above: View of the audience at the Isle of Wight Festival, estimated at 600,000, East Afton Down, Isle of Wight, August 1970.

began as a beautiful dream but it has got out of control and it is a monster.'

September

Barely three years after he set the music world – and his beloved Stratocaster – alight at the Monterey International Pop Festival, Jimi Hendrix died on 18 September, shortly after being found unconscious in his room at the Samarkand Hotel in London. The inquest held two weeks later recorded an open verdict on the death, which was described as being caused by 'inhalation of vomit due to barbiturate intoxication'. Just two days earlier, in what proved to be his final performance, the 27-year-old guitarist had jammed with Eric Burdon's band War on stage at Ronnie Scott's.

Hendrix had taken the electric guitar into areas other musicians could only dream of. Combining blues, jazz and funk rhythms with lengthy guitar improvisations that exploited feedback and distortion, he produced the soundtrack to the psychedelic explosion of the mid-1960s, and is still regarded as a genius – in 2003, he topped *Rolling Stone*'s list of the '100 greatest

1970 1971 1972 1973 1974 1975 1976 1977 1978 1979

Below: Jimi Hendrix playing the guitar at the Isle of Wight Festival.

1970 1971 1972 1973 1974 1975 1976 1977 1978 1979

guitarists of all time'. His death robbed the world of a unique talent whose work had transformed the sound of rock music forever – we can only imagine what he might have gone on to achieve had he lived...

October

Blues singer Janis Joplin became music's second big-name casualty of the year on 4 October, when her body was discovered in the Landmark Motor Hotel in Hollywood, California. She had died the day before from an overdose of heroin.

Joplin was, perhaps, the original 'wild child', rebelling from an early age against the conservatism of her hometown, Port Arthur in Texas. Dressing outrageously, drinking and swearing heavily, and later sleeping around, she was mostly shunned by her contemporaries, but eventually found her niche among the beatniks at the University of Texas playing blues and folk music in local clubs.

Like Hendrix, Joplin's big break came at Monterey in June 1967, where her performance with Big Brother and the Holding Company brought wide acclaim and kick-started her career. In the three years that followed, Joplin became a highly respected blues artist with Big Brother and her two subsequent outfits, the Kozmic Blues Band and the Full-Tilt Boogie Band. Her final recordings appeared on the posthumously-released album 'Pearl', including the prophetically-titled instrumental 'Buried Alive In The Blues', to which her vocals should have been added on the day she died.

SPORT

Mexico World Cup

The 1970 World Cup Finals in Mexico were the first where substitutes were allowed. Substitutes had been introduced in English football in 1965 to replace an injured player but it wasn't until 1967–68 that two were allowed for tactical reasons. The Finals were also the first to feature the lavish opening ceremony that has since become a tradition.

England went to Mexico as defending Champions, winning two of their three group games 1-0, against Romania and Czechoslovakia. Sandwiched between them was a 1-0 defeat at the hands of Brazil, a match best remembered for Gordon Banks's save from Pelé's header.

They met West Germany in the quarter-finals, who exacted revenge for the Final defeat four years earlier with a 3-2 extra-time victory. Sir Alf Ramsey had substituted Bobby Charlton and Martin Peters while 2-0 ahead and this would prove to be the last time Charlton graced an England shirt as he announced his international retirement after the tournament.

West Germany played out a classic match with Italy in an all-European semi-final while Brazil and Uruguay contested their own South American

Above: Brazilian captain Carlos Alberto smiles as he holds aloft the Jules Rimet Cup for Brazil in the World Cup Final, June 1970.
Below: Brazilian forward Pelé celebrates with his teammates.

version. In a seven-goal extra-time thriller, Italy edged into the Final while Brazil despatched Uruguay 3-1.

Brazil drew first blood when Pelé scored after 19 minutes but Boninsegna equalised for the Italians. Three second half goals from Gerson, Jairzinho and Carlos Alberto enabled Brazil to claim their third World Cup title and be awarded the trophy in perpetuity.

Manager Mario Zagallo became the first to win the trophy as both a player (1958 and 1962) and coach. He also coached them to the 1998 tournament in France but they lost to the host nation in the Final.

The 1970 tournament is fondly remembered for fair play and attacking football and not a single player was sent off.

Nijinsky II wins horseracing's English Triple Crown

Nijinsky II, son of Northern Dancer and Flaming Page, set the racing world alight in 1970 when he captured the English Triple Crown (of St Leger, 2,000 Guineas and Epsom Derby) for the first time since Bahrain in 1935 and legendary jockey Lester Piggott partnered him throughout.

Having been named Champion two-year-old in England and Ireland the previous season, Nijinsky won the 2,000 Guineas at Newmarket by two and a half lengths from Yellow God. Having won eight consecutive races from eight starts, he was entered in the Epsom Derby and again emerged victorious, this time with the fastest time since 1936.

An attack of ringworm hampered his training but owner Charles Engelhard overruled trainer Vincent O'Brien and Nijinsky entered the St Leger. He won by a length from Meadowville to enter the history books.

After two defeats, he was syndicated to the Claiborne Farm in Kentucky for a then world record of $5,440,000 and died in 1992.

Above: Lester Piggott riding 'Nijinsky'.

Margaret Court wins tennis Grand Slam

In 1970 Australian Margaret Court – one of the greatest tennis players the game has ever seen – became only the second woman to win the Grand Slam, matching Maureen 'Little Mo' Connolly's achievement 17 years earlier. Her doubles Grand Slam of 1963 makes her the only player – male or female – to have scored a clean sweep at both levels.

Born Margaret Smith on 16 July 1942 in Albury, New South Wales, she started off as a left-hander but then transferred the racquet to her other hand to dominate the world game between 1960–75, winning a record 62 Grand Slam titles (24 singles, 19 doubles and 19 mixed doubles). By comparison, the legendary Martina Navratilova is second in the list with 59.

She registered her first Grand Slam victory in her home tournament in 1960 when she was just 18, and she went on to retain the title another six times in succession, finishing with a record 11 Australian titles. She scored triples (singles, doubles, mixed titles) at the Australian in 1963, French 1964 and the US in 1970.

The 1970 Wimbledon Final has been labelled one of the best female matches of all time with Court, battling with a sprained ankle, overcoming Billie Jean King 14-12, 11-9 in a marathon meeting.

She had retired after the 1966 Wimbledon Championships and married Barry Court the following year before making her comeback in 1968. Her first and second children forced brief interludes in her career (1972 and 1974) but, expecting a third child, she retired permanently in 1977, having been ranked in the World Top Ten 13 times between 1961–75 (seven in the coveted Number 1 slot).

She was inducted into the International Tennis Hall of Fame in 1979 and has become a lay minister.

POLITICS & CURRENT AFFAIRS

Heath becomes Prime Minister

Even though the country had been going through a tough time and prime minister Harold Wilson had alienated a large swathe of the population, when he called a General Election in June 1970 few people expected anything other than another Labour victory. Opinion polls prior

Below: Margaret Court holds the Wimbledon women's singles trophy above her head after beating Billie Jean King in the Final.

1970 1971 1972 1973 1974 1975 1976 1977 1978 1979

to the event had suggested that Labour would be returned to power with a lead of at least 12%, but the pollsters had reckoned without a late swing towards the enigmatic Conservative leader Edward Heath.

Heath signified a change from traditional Tory leadership to a new 'middle class' approach, and this clearly went down well with the 'floating voters'. He was the son of a carpenter and a maid, and he had attended grammar school before going up to Balliol

Above: Edward Heath giving a victory wave as he arrives at Number Ten, after receiving his seal of office from the Queen.

18

College, Oxford. He later went into the army, and then became a civil servant, before entering politics. A talented musician and an accomplished yachtsman, he was very different to the old style Conservative leaders. The election gave Heath's Conservatives a total of 330 seats – 43 more than Labour and an overall majority of 31 seats in the new parliament. The 1970 General Election was also notable for ensuring that the Liberals, under new leader Jeremy Thorpe, lost half of the 12 seats they had previously held.

The election result was a shock to Wilson, but he retained leadership of the Labour Party and lived to fight another day. Heath was in many ways a very unusual man. He was a passionate pro-European, who had opposed the policy of appeasement before the Second World War. He never married and he was leader of the country for only four years, but in many ways he was unlucky. Noted for an appalling accent when speaking French, and for the fact that his shoulders shook violently whenever he laughed, Sir Edward Heath died in 2005, aged 89

De Gaulle Dies

Charles de Gaulle was born in Lille, in 1890. He was wounded three times in the First World War. He was then captured by the Germans and spent 32 months in prisoner of war camps, from which he made five unsuccessful escape attempts. As far as many French people were concerned, he attained heroic status during World War Two when, after seeing active service, he based himself in England as leader of the 'Free French'.

De Gaulle was nothing if not an imposing figure. He was 6 feet 5 inches tall, was possessed of a very large nose, and bore himself with an arrogance which was extreme, even by French standards. With the support of

Above: Portrait of the French general and first president of the Fifth Republic, Charles de Gaulle.

Winston Churchill, he was a focal point for French resistance during the latter part of the war, doing his best to unify the various resistance movements operating in France. After the liberation of his country, he became its leader, but resigned after only two months. He remained on the political scene, but later left it – before returning to be elected President in 1958.

De Gaulle's politics were distinctly right-wing. He decided that France should have its own nuclear bomb and, in 1966, he withdrew from the North Atlantic Treaty Organisation (NATO). He also repaid Britain for its wartime support, by continually blocking its attempts to join the EEC. 'Non' he said, and 'Non' he meant.

For all his faults, Charles de Gaulle was a brave man, and a true French patriot. He died on 9 November

Above: Headlines in a French newspaper announcing the death of Charles de Gaulle.

1970, having requested a private funeral with no orations or undue fuss. He was buried near his country home at Colombey-les-Deux Eglises, but his supporters were unable to stay away: tens of thousands of them lined the streets near the church to say a final adieu.

The Manson Murders

On 25 January 1970, Charles Manson, plus three co-defendants, were found guilty of murdering actress Sharon Tate and four others. The trial had lasted 121 days, and Manson himself was sentenced to life imprisonment. The story of Manson, who came from a classic deprived background, seemed at the time to be almost unbelievable. Having spent much of his young life engaged in criminal activities, and having been largely rejected by the music industry, Charles Manson had adopted a hippie, pseudo-religious, lifestyle and attracted followers who became known as 'The Family'. As leader of this strange cult, he then proceeded to instruct his followers to kill people – especially celebrities. Sharon Tate, wife of film director Roman Polanski, had been eight months pregnant at the time of her murder.

It became clear that Manson's followers had also committed earlier murders. His particular brand of evil shocked the United States, and indeed the whole world.

(LA5)LOS ANGELES, Dec.2--CULT LEADER?--Charles Manson, above 34, was described today by the Los Angeles Times and attorney Richard Caballero as the leader of a quasireligious cult of hippies, three of whom have been arrested on murder warrants issued in the slayings of actress Sharon Tate and four others at her home. Manson is in jail.

1970 1971 1972 1973 1974 1975 1976 1977 1978 1979

21

Above: Sharon Tate and her husband, Roman Polanski.
Below: Police mug shot of cult leader and murderer Charles Manson.

1971

FASHION, CULTURE & ENTERTAINMENT

The Novelty Song

Novelty songs performed by television celebrities whose fame was often enough to gain significant sales were particularly popular in the early 1960s. Usually heard on children's programmes such as *Crackerjack*, the songs were popular with pre-teenagers and their parents. Rolf Harris managed to get to Number 7 in the charts with 'Tie Me Kangaroo Down, Sport' in 1960 while Charlie Drake's 'My Boomerang Won't Come Back' reached Number 16 in 1961.

The following two years, however, saw the rise of the Beatles and the demise of the novelty song. But Christmas 1963 saw comedienne Dora Bryan reach Number 16 with 'All I Want For Christmas Is A Beatle'. A string of records by groups such as the Barron Knights parodying other chart numbers then followed.

By the early 1970s, novelty or comic records were back and 1971 became known for being the year of the 'naff' Number 1 – despite classic hits from T Rex, Rod Stewart and the Rolling Stones.

Clive Dunn, veteran actor of the hugely popular comedy classic *Dad's Army*, playing Lance-Corporal Jones, had a hit with 'Grandad' (he later went on to play Grandad in the children's TV series, 1979-84).

Comic actor Benny Hill had been performing in *The Benny Hill Show* since 1955, which sold to more than 140 countries worldwide. Hill worked as a milkman, bridge operator, driver and drummer before becoming an assistant stage manager. His huge success as a household name gave him a Christmas Number 1 in 1971 with 'Ernie, (The Fastest Milkman In The West)'.

Middle of the Road – a Scottish quartet who had got their break on the *Opportunity Knocks* programme a few years earlier – also got in on the act with 'Chirpy Chirpy Cheep Cheep' taking them to Number 1.

Above: Benny Hill, who had enormous success with 'Ernie'.

State University graphic design student Carolyn Davison to create a logo for the waffle sole 'Moon Shoe'.

Davidson presented a number of design options to Knight and other BRS executives, and they ultimately selected the 'Swoosh' logo. This first line of Nike (named after the Greek winged Goddess of victory) footwear was distributed to athletes competing in the US Olympic Track & Field Trials in Eugene, Oregon.

With first year sales of $8,000 the company went on to be one of the most successful sports manufacturing companies in the world. Today, Nike employs around 26,000 people worldwide and has 650,000 additional workers in Nike contracted factories. With a 12 per cent increase in revenue from the previous year and reported 2005 net revenues of $13.7 billion. In December 1980, Nike became a

Nike

Blue Ribbon Sports (BRS) was formed by Phil Knight (former middle-distance runner) and Bill Bowerman (former track and field coach) in the mid-1960s. In 1971 BRS needed a new brand of athletic footwear and asked Portland

Below: Examples of Nike shoes.

1970 1971 1972 1973 1974 1975 1976 1977 1978 1979

offices. In 1990, the first Niketown was opened in Portland, Oregon. Typically covering more than 30,000 square feet, Niketowns attract millions of customers every year and there are now a number of international Niketowns. October 2001 saw the launch of Nikegoddess, a store exclusively for women. Changing its name to Nikewoman in 2004, there are now more than 12 stores in the US, Canada and Europe.

The company strongly believes in human potential and has, over the years, set up subsidiaries that operate both within the sports industry and beyond. These companies include: Cole Haan Holdings Inc, Hurley International LLC, Nike IHM Inc, Bauer Nike Hockey, Exeter Brands Group LLC and Converse Inc.

Hot pants

Hot pants in 1971 were dressy shorts made from any material, although the most popular were velvet, satin and leather. They were so popular in 1971 that Royal Ascot had to relax its dress code, although ladies wearing hot pants were not allowed into the Royal Enclosure unless the entire outfit worn was deemed suitable for such an environment.

public company and is traded on the New York Stock Exchange (NYSE).

With facilities in Oregon, Tennessee, North Carolina and the Netherlands, Nike also operates leased facilities for 14 Niketowns, more than 2,000 factory stores, Nikewomen stores and sales and administrative

Although a short-lived fashion, they evoked the unconventional attitudes of the 1960s and were an adaptation of the mini skirt, offering the wearer more

Above: A couple getting married, she in the latest hot pants and boots.

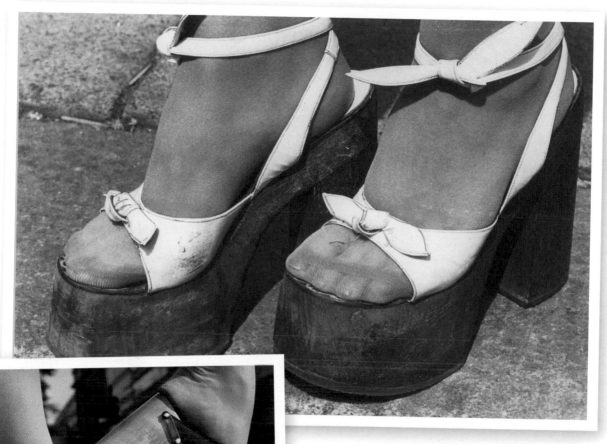

beneath maxi-length outfits. The open fronts and slits of maxi outfits enabled legs and hot pants to be visible and were considered trendy for the time. For those who wanted to reveal a little more, hot pants were a stylish solution.

Platform shoes

Thick, chunky platform shoes emerged in the early 1970s and it became acceptable for men, as well as women to wear them. This lack of gender rules helped distinguish the 1970s from earlier fashion eras. Platform shoes were emulated in pop art and by 1971 it was considered the most innovative year in shoe design.

From the disco to the office, platforms were everywhere and showed originality in design: suede, fruits, flowers, silver and multi-colours were strutting down virtually every street in the UK. The 1970s

modesty than the mini could provide. Hot pants were particularly popular for disco dancing.

They were designed to be worn as an item of clothing in its own right or as a revealed undergarment

1970 1971 1972 1973 1974 1975 1976 1977 1978 1979

Above and below: Platform shoes. The ones in the lower picture have eight inch heels.

1976 1979 1978 1977 1976 1975 1974 1973 1972 1971 1970

medical profession were increasingly worried about what damage was being done to the spines of the fashion conscious. In addition, soles and heels were so high that casualty departments nationwide were treating more and more patients who had sprained or broken ankles due to wearing them.

Space hopper

1971 seemed to be the year that all toys were round and dangerous. The space hopper was no exception. Despite the fact that you sat on it, held on tight and bounced up and down repeatedly until you either fell off, got a headache (from too much bouncing) or your hopper burst, the space hopper didn't really serve any purpose whatsoever. Yet, everyone had one – it was one of the most popular

celebrated the platforms' most psychedelic look. Platforms were so fashionable that most had at least two-inch soles and five-inch heels. The monstrous shoes worn by groups such as Kiss and artists like Elton John just contributed to the fever surrounding this outrageous fashion.

However, increased height in platforms caused medical issues. As fun as the shoes might have been they were impractical and uncomfortable and the

and recognisable toy crazes introduced that year.

Invented by Aquilino Cosani in the 1960s, the space hopper (also known as skippyball, hop ball, hoppity hop and kangaroo ball) was originally called the PON-PON, a rubber ball with a 60cm diameter. The elastic properties of the ball allow the person hopping to

Above: Marjorie McCoy, the British and World professional ice dance champion, on a spacehopper during Brighton toy fair.

move forward although in reality it was hard work. For those who miss their orange friend of yesteryear adult-sized versions are now available in the UK – joy of joys!

MUSIC

March

T Rex hit the top this month, when their single 'Hot Love' displaced Mungo Jerry's 'Baby Jump' to give them their first UK Number 1. Less than a week later, *Radio 1 Club* broadcast a T Rex session that included the new single alongside two tracks from the recently-released 'T Rex' album, itself enjoying a chart run that would eventually last for almost half the year.

The T Rex bandwagon was really gathering pace – just a year earlier, Marc Bolan and Mickey Finn were performing mainly acoustic material to a largely hippy audience under the Tyrannosaurus Rex banner, but the release of 'Ride A White Swan' in the autumn of 1970 marked a change in direction.

Below: Mickey Finn (left) with singer, songwriter and guitarist Marc Bolan.

REMEMBER THE SEVENTIES

A simple electric bass line and a smattering of strings were added to the mix, and the result was an irresistible, catchy song that gave Bolan his first real taste of chart success. Only Clive Dunn's novelty hit 'Grandad' prevented it from reaching the coveted top spot.

This new approach brought about some big changes – to reproduce the new, fuller sound in concert, Bolan recruited bassist Steve Currie and drummer Bill Legend, and the classic T Rex line-up was complete. T Rex were set to become one of the biggest pop phenomena of the early 1970s,

and over the next two years it seemed they could do no wrong.

It wasn't just the music that caused such a stir – Bolan's flamboyant clothes and the glittery eye make-up he wore for the band's *Top Of The Pops* appearances were all part of the appeal to the next generation of record-buyers, and almost overnight a new musical genre was born – 'glam rock'. The effect was widespread and almost immediate – within weeks, the shops were full of vivid, glittering silks and satins, setting the tone for the most colourful summer since 1967.

Below: Mick Jagger and Bianca Perez Morera de Macias in Saint Tropez during their Civil wedding ceremony.

May

The St Tropez marriage of Mick Jagger and Bianca Perez Morena de Macias brought every A-list rock celebrity to the south of France. Ex-Beatles McCartney and Starr, Eric Clapton, Stephen Stills and, of course, the other Rolling Stones were on hand to toast the bride and groom with a glass of rock'n'roll mouthwash (champers to the rest of us) as they went through a civil service at the Town Hall, then a Roman Catholic church service.

At the latter, a selection of tunes from the film *Love Story* was played on a harmonium, apparently at the bride's request. Her husband had previously thrown a tantrum at the number of photographers present at the Town Hall, complaining he didn't want to get married in a 'fish bowl'. He'd relented enough by the reception to get up on stage with soul divas PP Arnold and Doris Troy for an impromptu set.

An additional wedding present for grumpy Mick arrived at the end of the month when the band achieved the rare feat of topping both the US single and album charts with 'Brown Sugar' and parent LP 'Sticky Fingers'.

July

Another late-1960s rock icon bowed out early this month, when former Doors frontman Jim Morrison was found dead in the bath in a Paris apartment. Morrison, who like Jimi Hendrix and Janis Joplin, died at the age of 27, was staying in Paris with his

partner Pamela Courson. Despite making his name as a vocalist, Morrison always regarded himself first and foremost as a poet, and had recently announced his intention to take a break from the band to concentrate on writing.

Mystery surrounds his death to this day – officially, he died of heart failure, but only two people, Pamela and the French doctor she summoned to the apartment, saw the body, and no autopsy was ever performed. Over the years fans have perpetuated rumours that the death was faked, or that it was related to Morrison's interest in the occult. Whatever

Above: The grave of Jim Morrison strewn with flowers.

1970 1971 1972 1973 1974 1975 1976 1977 1978 1979

the truth, the enigma of his final hours was entirely in keeping with the man's love of rich, mysterious imagery.

September

One of the most influential rock shows of all time made its debut this month in the shape of *The Old Grey Whistle Test*. Its no-frills style was then unique, and in stark contrast to the glitter and glamour of programmes like *Top Of The Pops*, but it soon proved to be a great success, and its influence can clearly be seen in

subsequent shows such as *Later with Jools Holland*, *The Tube* and *The White Room*.

With the show's commitment to new music, bands would often be making their first TV appearance. These were the days before 24-hour TV, and the show aired last thing on a Friday night, giving it a degree of flexibility. If things were going well, the programme would be allowed to run on, sometimes for as much as 90 minutes.

Originally presented by Richard Williams, the *Whistle Test* would, from 1972, become the domain of

Above: Bob Harris, presenter of the BBC television programme 'The Old Grey Whistle Test', drapes his arm around female vocalist Maggie Bell.

'Whispering' Bob Harris. And no-one who regularly watched the show can ever forget that title sequence, which featured an animation of a man kicking a star – affectionately known as the 'Starkicker' – over a track called 'Stone Fox Chase' by Nashville band Area Code 615.

SPORT

Arsenal win Double

With North London rivals Spurs having achieved the first Double (League and FA Cup) of the twentieth century ten years earlier, Arsenal fans were overjoyed that they could equal that feat.

The season kicked off away to League Champions Everton and goals from Charlie George and George Graham gave the Gunners a creditable 2-2 draw. The first defeat of the season came at Chelsea on 29 August, a 2-1 reverse with Eddie Kelly netting for the visitors. A 6-2 thrashing of West Bromwich Albion in September preceded a 5-0 thumping at the hands of Stoke City, a team who would give Arsenal a torrid time in the FA Cup.

The Highbury outfit then embarked on a 14-match unbeaten League run that propelled them up the table. Indeed, they would only lose four more times that season (away to Huddersfield Town, Liverpool, Derby County and Leeds United) en route to the Division One title.

Below: Team captain Frank McLintock and goalkeeper Bob Wilson lift the trophy for Arsenal after they beat Liverpool 2-1 in the FA Cup Final at Wembley Stadium.

1970 1971 1972 1973 1974 1975 1976 1977 1978 1979

1970 1971 1972 1973 1974 1975 1976 1977 1978 1979

The key to this success was the meagre pickings opposing teams could glean from the defence: marshalled by keeper Bob Wilson, the Gunners kept an awesome 25 clean sheets in 42 League games conceding only 29 goals.

The FA Cup run started in the Third Round against Yeovil Town but there was no chance of a giant killing as the non-League minnows were despatched 3-0. Replays were required to get past Portsmouth (Fourth Round) and Leicester City (Sixth Round) to set up a Semi-Final meeting with Stoke City at Hillsborough.

Again, Arsenal could not find the winning strike, with two Kelly strikes earning them a 2-2 draw and a replay at St Andrews. This time, however, the Gunners made no mistake with goals from Graham and George easing their passage to Wembley with a 2-0 victory.

Liverpool were their Cup Final opponents and the mercurial Charlie George went down in Highbury history, scoring the extra-time winner in a 2-1 triumph.

Ibrox disaster

For a football ground to endure one disaster with loss of life is tragic, for that same ground to witness two such incidents beggars belief. But that is exactly the fate that befell Glasgow Rangers' Ibrox Stadium.

A stand collapsed during the 1902 Home International between Scotland and England leading to 26 deaths but

Above: Action during a test match on the British Lions Tour of New Zealand in 1971.
Below: A section of the terracing which collapsed at Ibrox Park in Glasgow, in the first Ibrox disaster of 1902.

32

players and club officials to attend each funeral and the city of Glasgow united to aid the victims' families with a benefit match being staged between Scotland and a Rangers-Celtic XI.

Lions tour Australia/ New Zealand and become only Lions side to win in NZ

The British Lions' 1971 Tour of Australia and New Zealand proved to be the most successful ever, with the Lions registering their only Test series victory against the All Blacks on their own turf.

With Wales winning the 1971 Grand Slam, it was understandable that they provided the

this pales in comparison to the events of the 2 January 1971 Old Firm derby.

Originally believed to have occurred because a late Rangers equaliser caused spectators to reverse their direction up Stairway 13, it has since been recorded that it was the sheer numbers descending the stairwell that led to the crush in which 66 people lost their lives and around 200 were injured.

Manager Willie Waddell requested permission from each bereaved family for his

Below: Portrait of JPR Williams.

1970 1971 1972 1973 1974 1975 1976 1977 1978 1979

majority of the Lions squad with 14 players being selected. Seven players were chosen from England, and six from both Scotland and Ireland to complete the 33-man squad.

The tour kicked off after a marathon flight with defeat against Queensland (11-15) quickly followed by a 14-12 victory over New South Wales despite a poor performance. Further warm-up matches followed against provincial sides and included convincing victories over Wellington (47-9) and West Coast/Buller (39-6) in the run up to the first Test.

New Zealand were despatched 9-3 in Dunedin with Scottish loosehead prop Ian McLauchlan scoring the only try of the game. Buoyed by this result, the Lions were brought down to earth in the second Test with a 12-22 mauling in Christchurch.

Wellington was the venue for the third Test three weeks later and tries from Gerald Davies and Barry John helped the Lions to a 13-3 triumph to claim a 2-1 lead going into the last match.

Auckland saw the Lions only needing to draw to win the series and at half-time the scores were level

Below: A computer tape machine in the computer room of the Open University, 1971.

at 8-8, England flanker Peter Dixon going over for the Lions' sole try. Barry John scored from a penalty to give the visitors the advantage but the All Blacks soon levelled to set up a nailbiting finish. Welsh full-back JPR Williams stunned everyone with a 45-metre drop goal and New Zealand could only respond with a penalty to tie the game at 14-14.

Of the 26 games the Lions played on the 1971 Tour, they won 23, drew one and only lost two and returned home to a hero's welcome.

POLITICS & CURRENT AFFAIRS

Open University

The Open University, which was originally to be known as the University of the Air, came into being in January 1971. It was a pet project of former prime minister Harold Wilson, and although it had been reviled by many in Conservative circles, it took on its first students while the Tories were in power. The OU was conceived as a means of providing further education for those who had not obtained the basic qualifications whilst at school, and initially it was only available to mature students – although this was changed in 1974. 'Distance learning' was to be employed, with students undertaking most of the work from home, and the BBC was to become heavily involved with the production of Open University programmes.

The Open University has had its critics over the years, but from the beginning it was largely a success story. By the time of its first degree ceremony in 1973, a thousand students had sat final exams, with 867 of them having passed.

Above: Prime Minister, Harold Wilson, making a speech. In the background, far right, is Jenny Lee, widow of Aneurin Bevan who was influential in setting up the Open University.

The vice chancellor, Dr. Walter Perry, insisted in 1973 that the degrees were on a par with those of the best universities in the country. He also said, 'The qualities of our students are often very different. In the first place they are adult, experienced in life and jobs, not just straight out of school.'

By 1973 the OU had some 40,000 students on its books. This figure has since risen to almost 200,000, with many students residing outside the United Kingdom. There is a higher than average failure rate, with some 30 per cent either dropping out or otherwise failing to obtain a degree, but there can be no doubt that the University of the Air has given a second chance to many thousands of people who thought that they would never be able to aspire to studying at a higher level.

Above: A pamphlet introducing the decimal currency.
Middle: The publicity campaign explaining the complexities of decimal currency.

Decimalisation Day

Britain's currency had been based on the duo decimal system for hundreds of years. Everyone knew that there were twelve pennies in a shilling and, for that matter,

that twenty shillings made a pound. Most people knew that there were twenty-one shillings in a guinea, although it must be admitted that some had forgotten that there were once three groats to the shilling. Still, it was all very simple until,

in preparation for entry into the European Economic Community, the government decided to make it even simpler. Shillings would be abolished, as for that matter would tanners, threepenny bits, and ten bob notes, and the United Kingdom would enter the brave new world of decimalisation.

There was much discussion about a proposed new currency, with a new unit, worth ten shillings, being at first favoured in place of the pound. Of course, ten shillings would have to be called something else,

Below: A display showing the new decimal coinage.

1970 1971 1972 1973 1974 1975 1976 1977 1978 1979

possibly – horror of horrors – a dollar, so this idea was abandoned. Britain was joining Europe, not the USA.

D-Day was finally set for 15 February 1971. Henceforth there would be 100 new pennies to the pound, the new penny being worth exactly 2.4 old pennies. No conversion problems there, then. In fact, people quite quickly adapted to the new money. There were fears that traders would take the opportunity to surreptitiously raise prices, and a few did, but on the whole things went smoothly. Naturally, many traditionalists still hated the new currency. The new halfpennies were too small, and there was a general

feeling that everyone was being short-changed. A campaign to save the old sixpence, or tanner, which was conveniently worth exactly 2.5 new pence, meant that this coin was retained in circulation for some years. In time however, the Great British Public largely forgot about the old money, although fifty pence pieces were for years referred to by some as 'ten bob bits'.

Rolls-Royce Bankrupt

When Mr Rolls and Mr Royce began manufacturing motor cars in 1906, their aim was to produce only the very best of vehicles. It was said that a Rolls-Royce

Above: In production at Rolls-Royce, Derby, are these 48,000lb thrust RB 211-524 engines.

engine could barely be heard above the ticking of the car's clock, and for many years the marque was synonymous with excellence and luxury.

However, by the late 1920s, aircraft engines were to form the core of the company's business, and it was an aircraft engine which was to bring Rolls-Royce to its knees. The company invested heavily in the production of the RB 211 engine for the Lockheed TriStar widebody passenger jet, and it all went horribly wrong. Rolls-Royce was declared bankrupt in February 1971 and, in order to save it, Edward Heath's Conservative government ordered its nationalisation. The company was later privatised again by Margaret Thatcher.

1970 1971 1972 1973 1974 1975 1976 1977 1978 1979

Above: A production-built, Rolls-Royce RB 211 three-shaft turbofan power unit.

1972

FASHION, CULTURE & ENTERTAINMENT

Cosmopolitan takes Britain by storm

Cosmopolitan, a young women's magazine, began life in the US in 1886 as a fiction magazine. By 1965 its circulation was in decline and its advertising sales waning. Helen Gurley Brown turned the magazine around and today it is a household name which can boast a significant role in shaping the lives of young women around the globe while remaining the number one magazine in its genre.

Gurley Brown, a former advertising copywriter who had written a best seller – *Sex And The Single Girl* – approached the Hearst Corporation (a leading US company in publishing, communications and broadcasting) about the possibility of a new type of magazine based on her book advising young women about how to lead hectic lives, cope with relationships and have successful jobs. Gurley Brown had celebrity status, was innovative and creative and had the ability to use directness in the magazine which reached out to thousands of young women looking for self-improvement. More than one million copies of the first issue were sold (within ten years the readership would grow to 2.5 million) and it was decided to launch a UK edition.

National Magazines (Natmags) were given six months' notice that they would be launching the new *Cosmo* in Britain. Woman's editor at *The Sun*, Joyce Hopkirk, was chosen as UK editor while Deirdre McSharry was given the role of fashion and beauty editor. With a total of six staff, the new magazine was

launched in March 1972 with little-known Saatchi & Saatchi responsible for advertising.

The magazine's hype was huge and speculation that the second issue would include a male nude meant that the publication was rarely out of the news. However, some of the directness lapped up by consumers was not so well received in other areas. *The Daily Mail*

was shocked by the word virgin appearing in an advert, while London Transport insisted that the word 'frigid' be covered on adverts used on public transport with a black strip. Unfortunately the strips were not long enough and many adverts sported the words "I was f.....d".

The Osmonds

Osmond-mania hit the UK in 1972 when two members of The Osmonds, a US singing family who became a worldwide phenomenon, topped the charts with their solo efforts. Donny Osmond (14) enjoyed a five-week

Above: 'Cosmopolitan' editor Helen Gurley Brown.

stay at Number 1 with 'Puppy Love' in July and nine year old 'Little' Jimmy captured hearts with 'Long Haired Lover From Liverpool'. That also sat atop the charts for five weeks at the end of the year.

October inevitably saw the first UK visit by the family, who flew into Heathrow prior to their appearance on the Royal Variety Show. The visit had been the subject of an unprecedented media build-up, and the boys – Alan, Wayne, Merrill and Jay, the original quartet, plus Donny and Jimmy – arrived to find more than 8,000 screaming girls waiting to greet them. One year later,

By the end of 1972, they had no less than three singles in the UK Top 20 – Donny's 'Why', Little Jimmy's 'Long Haired Lover…', and the whole family's 'Crazy Horses', a protest song against automotive pollution.

Though they inspired hysteria not seen since the Beatles, The Osmonds, devout Mormons, had always been seen in the States as safe and family-oriented. Having had a lucky break at Disneyland, the family became regular guests on *The Andy Williams Show* during the 1960s. In 1972, ABC gave them a Saturday morning cartoon series which ran until the following year, while sister Marie later teamed up with Donny to achieve worldwide success with *The Donny and Marie Show*.

Roller skates

In 1743 roller skates were recorded as having been used in a London stage performance. It is not known who invented the particular skates used, but Jean-Joseph Merlin was recorded to have invented an inline

when the Osmonds flew into Heathrow again, tragedy was only narrowly avoided when part of a balcony railing collapsed and 18 young girl fans were injured in the resulting crush.

The toothy idols dominated teen magazines and peppered the UK charts with a succession of hit singles.

Above: The Osmonds.
Below: A pair of 'Super Skates'.

skate with metal wheels in 1760. Early skates were similar to modern inline skates, but early skaters were unable to do anything other than move in a straight line or make sweeping turns.

By 1972, the roller skating craze had exploded in the UK and Raquel Welch starred on a pair in *Kansas*

City Bomber about a female derby player learning to take control of her life both on and off the track. Between 1955 and the mid-1970s roller skating was a popular contact sport in the US played at both professional and amateur levels featuring teams of both men and women. Two teams of five skate on a banked track trying to score points by lapping their opponents. However, like professional wrestling with its good guy/bad guy mentality, staged brawls were the order of the day ensuring as much entertainment as possible for the audience.

Loon pants

Loon pants had their heyday during the early to mid-1970s (anyone seen wearing a pair post-1975 was

likely to get a good beating). Hip-hugging trousers which flared out from the knee into a huge bell-bottom that consumed feet were extremely popular by 1972 at a time when fashion was keeling from the sublime to the ridiculous.

Usually made of crushed velvet, denim or corduroy, the baggy trousers were all the rage. Loon pants were popular with hippies who could initially buy them by postal order. The style was to wear your pants with a Led Zeppelin T-shirt and Jesus boots.

The Godfather

Starring Marlon Brando, Al Pacino, James Caan and Diane Keaton, *The Godfather* – written and adapted

Above: A hippy wearing a knitted skullcap and flared loon pants.

clash of the Don's old fading values. The new ways demand a terrible price from Michael for the sake of the whole family.

MUSIC

March

Marc Bolan's career hit its peak this month when the boppin' elf made a triumphant appearance at the Empire Pool, Wembley. Tickets, priced at 75p, went on sale on 18 February, and sold out within days. An additional matinee performance was added, and this, too, sold out in double-quick time – 'T Rextasy', as Bolan's publicist BP Fallon described it, was in full effect.

The Empire Pool had not previously been associated with rock gigs, but the need for a bigger venue to allow thousands of T Rex fans to see their idol had made it an ideal choice, and in the months that followed the Moody Blues, Pink Floyd and the Grateful Dead all played there, confirming it as the UK's number one indoor arena.

Bolan was inescapable for the rest of the year – he was interviewed, photographed and quoted as if no-one else mattered. All this attention proved to be his downfall – finally acknowledged as the superstar he always aspired to be, Bolan began to lose the plot. His former self-confidence turned into an overarching smugness, and he alienated many of those who'd helped him on the road to success.

As Bolan's stock fell, one of his earlier admirers stood poised to take over. 1972 proved to be the breakthrough year for David Bowie, whose 'Ziggy Stardust' album was greeted with rave reviews in June.

from his own novel by Mario Puzo and directed by Francis Ford Coppola – is as huge today as it was when it was first screened in 1972.

'Don' Vito Corleone, played by Brando, is the head of a New York Mafia family. His daughter is getting married and his son, Michael (Al Pacino), has just returned home from the war and is not intending to become part of his father's business empire. Seen through Michael's life, a picture of the family and its 'business' soon becomes clear. Kind and benevolent to those who show respect, the family is ruthless and violent to anyone who stands in their way or who goes against the greater good of the family. A Corleone family rival wants to start selling drugs in New York, sparking a

Above: Marlon Brando, in character as mob kingpin Don Vito Corleone from the film 'The Godfather'.

1970 1971 1972 1973 1974 1975 1976 1977 1978 1979

1976 1978 1977 1976 1975 1974 1973 1972 1971 1970

In August, his show at London's Rainbow Theatre was a sell-out, and Bowie became the new Glam Rock sensation, although he still looked up to Bolan. 'Ziggy Stardust' included the song 'Lady Stardust', written about Marc, and when the song was played live, Bowie performed it in front of a projected image of Bolan's face. Bolan's music was also played in concert halls

before Bowie took the stage, effectively reversing the situation of several years earlier, when Bowie had opened shows for the two-piece Tyrannosaurus Rex.

August

Soon after Wembley's Empire Pool played host to its first rock concert, Wembley Stadium itself got in on the act. In August, over 80,000 fans gathered beneath the twin towers to witness the first Rock'n'Roll Revival show,

featuring many of the biggest names from the Fifties. Bill Haley, Chuck Berry, Little Richard and Jerry Lee Lewis topped the bill, but before the fans got to see

their idols, there were warm up acts including Screaming Lord Sutch, Gary Glitter, America's MC5 and the debut appearance of Roy Wood's new band, Wizzard.

The rock'n'roll equivalent of Woodstock lasted over 11 hours, but boasted few real highlights – none of the old guard was on particularly good form, and the audience of Teddy Boys and Rockers gave some of the performers a rough time. Mind you, the 'Kings of Rock'n'Roll' themselves were no less scathing about each other – interview footage recorded at the event shows Little Richard describing Jerry Lee Lewis as 'The King of Stupidity', while Lewis retorts that he hasn't 'seen any hit records by Little Richard lately'...

Above right: David Bowie in costume as 'Ziggy Stardust'.
Below: Marc Bolan in action at the Empire Pool, Wembley.

August

John Lennon, a New York resident for the past year despite his immigration visa expiring in February, played his first official American concert this month at Madison Square Garden. In fact, he enjoyed it so much he played two!

Backed by sprawling jazz-rock ensemble Elephant's Memory, who'd also appeared on their just-released 'Sometime In New York City', John and Yoko Ono offered an eclectic set that included a version of the Beatles' 'Come Together' and a cover of Elvis Presley's 'Hound Dog' as well as four solo efforts from Mro Lonnon. The gigs, charity benefits which raised $250,000 for the city's Willowbrook Hospital, also featured Sha Na Na, Stevie Wonder and Roberta Flack, perhaps inevitably climaxed with a communal version of the Lennon anthem 'Give Peace A Chance'.

A selection of the songs performed would be released some years after his death as 'John Lennon: Live In New York City'.

Meanwhile, former partner Paul McCartney was getting into trouble in Gothenburg, Sweden. As his group Wings left the stage at the Scandinavium Hall, he and wife Linda, together with drummer Denny Seiwell,

Above: Hippies and rockers together at the rock 'n' roll Revival Show, held at Wembley Stadium.
Below: A group of teddy boys dancing at the London rock'n'roll revival show in Wembley.

1970 1971 1972 1973 1974 1975 1976 1977 1978 1979

for a four-week stay with a bizarre near-instrumental single. 'Mouldy Old Dough' was the product of Lieutenant Pigeon, a group from Coventry featuring drummer Nigel Fletcher, pianist Robert Woodward and bassist Steve Johnson. Having had no luck as Staveley Makepeace, they enlisted Woodward's piano-teacher mum Hilda and changed their name for this hit, recorded in the front room of their semi-detached home. The only vocal on the record was the repetition of the title.

Theirs was a one-off success, though the sound-alike 'Desperate Dan' did make it to the Top 20 before the Pigeon plummeted. They nevertheless became the first group to top the UK chart with a mother and son in the same group.

December

Two rock-based big-screen offerings were released to very different receptions this month. Marc Bolan's glam reign hit a hiccup when his self-indulgent feature film, *Born To Boogie*, directed by ex-Beatle Ringo Starr, premiered at Oscar One in London's Soho. While the Wembley Arena shows in March at which it was filmed (his last British gigs for 18 months, as it transpired) were described by *Melody Maker* as a 'New Peak of Bolan Mania', the resulting movie was panned by *New Musical Express* as 'bad, atrocious, cheap, pretentious, narcissistic and noisy.'

Meanwhile, as Pink Floyd prepared their magnum opus, 'Dark Side Of The Moon', for March release, they sent their feature film *Live At Pompeii* around the cinemas in their stead. A lot less bombastic than Bolan's effort, being a concert

were taken to one side and arrested for drugs possession. A parcel addressed to the ex-Beatle containing seven ounces of marijuana had been intercepted at customs, leading police to the band's dressing room. 'This will make good publicity for our concerts,' a member of the entourage was reported to have quipped, and certainly 'Fab Macca' could afford to laugh off his £800 fine.

Unfortunately, the McCartneys would be busted again at their Scottish farm the following month when cannabis plants were found growing in a greenhouse, an event doubtless designed to publicise their forthcoming single release 'Hi Hi Hi'! History would repeat itself with a bust in Japan in 1980, since which time Sir Paul has managed to keep his nose clean...

October

On 14 October 1972, the strangest quartet the pop world had seen in many a moon ascended to Number 1

Above: Paul and Linda McCartney with members of their pop group Wings.

There were changes to the schedule with archery and handball being included for the first time in 52 years and 36 years respectively. Munich also saw the introduction of slalom or white-water canoeing.

American Mark Spitz was the undoubted star of the Games as he swam his way to a record seven gold medals but it was 17-year-old Olga Korbut who captured the hearts of the watching world. The tiny Russian gymnast won two individual gold medals,

performance filmed in an old Roman amphitheatre, it pulled in the plaudits.

SPORT

Munich Olympics

The 1972 Summer Olympic Games held in Munich will unfortunately be most remembered for events that unfolded away from the sporting arenas. On 5 September, Arab terrorists broke into the compound housing the Israeli athletes, killing two and taking nine hostages. In the ensuing gun battle, all the hostages were killed and the Games were suspended while a memorial service took place.

1970 1971 1972 1973 1974 1975 1976 1977 1978 1979

47

Above: Opening ceremony of the Munich Olympics.
Below left: Olga Korbut proudly displays one of her two gold medals.
Below right: Mark Spitz celebrates winning his fifth gold medal, in the 100 metres butterfly, at the 1972 Munich Olympics.

1970 1971 1972 1973 1974 1975 1976 1977 1978 1979

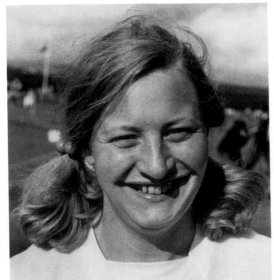

Bobby Fischer becomes first US World Chess Champion

Bobby Fischer first burst onto the world chess scene in 1956 when – as a 13-year-old – he took part in what has since been labelled the Game of the Century against fellow American Donald Byrne.

Fischer, born on 9 March 1943, became the United States' first World Chess Champion when he defeated Russian master Boris Spassky on 1 September 1971.

one team gold and an individual silver at her first Olympics.

There was controversy involving the US team: Vince Matthews and Wayne Collett – gold and silver medallists in the 400 metres – were banned for life after fooling around on the rostrum during the American national anthem, and the basketball team found themselves on the losing side for the first time and refused to accept their silver medals following Russia's last-minute 51-50 victory.

British successes included Mary Peters, who registered a world record points score in the pentathlon. Brian Jacks claimed bronze in the Middleweight judo and boxer Alan Minter won the Light Middleweight bronze at the start of glittering careers. The Great Britain teams successfully defended their gold medals in the yachting Flying Dutchman class and the Equestrian Three Day Eventing. Richard Meade won the individual Three Day Event gold and hurdler David Hemery claimed a bronze to go with his gold from four years earlier.

Losing the first game and defaulting the second by not turning up did not bode well but Fischer won the third game and Spassky only won once more, the match eventually finishing after the 21st game with a 12.5-8.5 scoreline.

Above: Mary Peters, winner of a gold medal for Britain in the Pentathlon event at the 1972 Munich Olympics.
Below: American world chess Champion Bobby Fischer.

Fischer continued his erratic behaviour by turning up for the award ceremony an hour late but has been credited with bringing many innovations to the game. He remained World Champion until 1975 when he refused to defend his title and he did not play chess again in public until 1992.

Higgins wins world title

When Alex Higgins won snooker's World Championship in 1972, he became the youngest person to claim the prestigious trophy in its 55-year history. (This was eclipsed in 1991 by the 21-year old Stephen Hendry.)

Born on 18 March 1949 in Belfast, Northern Ireland, Alexander Gordon Higgins won the All-Ireland and Northern Ireland Amateur Championships in 1968, turning professional three years later. Winning the world title at the first attempt was a dream few can ever

hope to aspire to but that is exactly what Higgins, nicknamed 'Hurricane' because of his quick playing style, achieved in 1972.

Held at Birmingham's Selly Park British Legion, Higgins overcame Jackie Rea 19-11 in his first round match and defeated former World Champion John Pulman 31-23 in the quarter-final. The semi-final against Rex Williams – the reigning World Professional Billiards Champion – proved to be a close-fought affair. Williams moved into a commanding 12-6 frame advantage before Higgins fought back to lead 26-25. Tied at 30 frames apiece going into the last, it took Higgins to the green to book his place in the Final.

Twice-world Champion John Spencer was the pre-match favourite and the final obstacle for Higgins to overcome. He achieved this early in the final session to take the title by 37 frames to 32 and claim the prize money of just over £400…a far cry from the £200,000 pot on offer to the winner of the 2006 tournament.

Higgins went on to reach three more World Championship Finals, losing to Ray Reardon in 1976 and Cliff Thorburn four years later before regaining his title with a 18-15 victory over Reardon in 1982 that included an impressive 135 total clearance in the final frame.

Now semi-retired, Higgins has battled throat cancer in recent years and is said to have blown most of the £3 million he earned from snooker.

POLITICS & CURRENT AFFAIRS

Miners' Strike

Following an overtime ban by British coal miners, which had cost the industry an estimated £20 million in lost revenue, the miners went on strike on 9 January 1972. It was the first national coal strike for almost fifty years, and although there was initially quite a lot of support

Above: Alex Higgins.

1970 1971 1972 1973 1974 1975 1976 1977 1978 1979

average 21 per cent wage increase was reached, and the strike was called off from 25 February. The coal miners had won the battle, but they were eventually to lose the war. Further disruption in subsequent years was to contribute eventually to the demise of the mining industry and the destruction of mining communities across the country.

for the strikers, the dispute was soon to bring the nation to its knees.

The miners believed that the dangers and difficulties of their work had never been properly recognised, and they were demanding a pay rise of up to 35 per cent. This would take their net pay from an average of £25 a week to about £34, and make them the country's highest paid manual workers. Unfortunately, the Conservative government had recently imposed an unofficial pay ceiling of 8 per cent, so there seemed little room for compromise. Derek Ezra, the chairman of the Coal Board, was adamant that the miners' claim could not be met. After the strike had been called, he said: 'The only way of recouping the money would then have been to put prices up, and we would have had to put the price of coal up by at least another 15 per cent.'

The miners' strike lasted for seven weeks. Coal stocks began to run dangerously low and, on 9 February, a State of Emergency was declared. A three-day working week was announced and 1.2 million workers were eventually laid off. The economic situation worsened and, in the end, the government was largely forced to give in. A settlement, giving the miners an

Bloody Sunday

There had been renewed trouble in Northern Ireland since 1968, and it came to a head on 30 January 1972, on what became known as Bloody Sunday. A

Above: Donations of food to Kent coal miners during a strike.
Below: Coffins of 11 victims of the 'Bloody Sunday' massacre are carried out of St Mary's church on Creggan Hill in Derry City, following a Requiem Mass.

the reckless' but that they had indeed been fired upon first – something the marchers have always denied.

The events of Bloody Sunday led to even greater unrest in the province, and to yet greater distrust between the two communities. Three days after the shootings, the British Embassy in Dublin was burnt down, and in February IRA bombs claimed three lives at Aldershot barracks. The British government, led by a beleaguered Edward Heath, decided that enough was enough. Power was removed from Northern Ireland's Stormont parliament, and in its place direct rule from Westminster was imposed. It was far from being the end of the troubles in Northern Ireland.

march from Londonderry's Creggan Estate was organised by Catholics and Republicans, as a way of protesting against the imposition of internment without trial. Around 10,000 people gathered for what was technically an illegal protest, with the intention of taking part in a city centre rally. As with most marches, everything started off peacefully enough, but when British paratroopers sealed off part of the route, trouble inevitably ensued. Stones and other missiles were thrown at them, and at first the troops responded with rubber bullets, CS gas and water cannon.

The soldiers had been instructed to make arrests, but they ended up using conventional ammunition and shot 13 people dead. The paratroopers claimed they were fired upon first, while the marchers claimed the soldiers had started the firing and had murdered unarmed civilians. The Inquiry under Lord Widgery, which took many years and cost a reputed £150 million, found that the soldiers' firing had 'bordered on

Amin expels Asians

Due to his ludicrous posturing and obvious insanity, Idi Amin became a figure of fun in Britain. He was however a ruthless and brutal dictator, who ruled Uganda from 1971 until overthrown in 1979. Having himself overthrown Ugandan president Milton Obote, Amin declared himself 'president for life' and proceeded to become responsible for the murder of hundreds of thousands of his own people. His regime was totally despotic. In 1972 he ordered the expulsion of his country's Asian population, accusing those of Asian origin of controlling the economy for their own ends. Many of them fled to Britain, where they did well – while Uganda fell into economic chaos.

Upon his overthrow, Amin found sanctuary in Saudi Arabia. He was never to be put on trial for any of his horrific crimes, and the world largely forgot about him. He died in Saudi in 2003.

Above: Ugandan soldier, dictator and head of state, General Idi Amin.

1970 1971 1972 1973 1974 1975 1976 1977 1978 1979

1979 1978 1977 1976 1975 1974 **1973** 1972 1971 1970

1973

FASHION, CULTURE & ENTERTAINMENT

Bruce Lee dies

Martial arts star Bruce Lee, dressed in a traditional Chinese outfit was buried in Lakeview Cemetery Seattle in late July 1973. A certain amount of mystery and unanswered questions still surround his death.

The facts are that he died in the apartment of Betty Tingpei, a Taiwanese actress with whom he had just had a meeting (along with film producer Raymond Chow) about the making of the film *Game Of Death*. After complaining of a headache, Lee had taken a pill and fallen asleep at Tingpei's home. He died after falling into a coma and while the coroner's report was inconclusive, medical authorities came up with five reasons for his death. All agreed it was caused by a cerebral edema (a swelling of the brain caused by a congestion of fluid).

Bruce Lee was the iconic figure of martial arts cinema. Had it not been for his remarkable movies in the first few years of the 1970s, it's unlikely martial arts would have had the impact they did on popular culture. Audiences worldwide continue to enjoy this movie genre.

Lee was a phenomenon whose influence can be seen in many other film genres including comedy, action, drama, science-fiction, horrors and animation. Born in November 1940 in San Francisco, Lee's family returned to Kowloon, Hong Kong in 1941. At the age of five, Lee was appearing in minor films and after having been beaten up some years later was inspired to take up martial arts. Trained by 'Sifu Yip Man' for five years in wing chun kung fu, Lee also took up cha-cha

dancing, winning a major dance competition. After falling foul of the local police his parents suggested that he return to the US where he opened kung fu training schools.

He was introduced to TV producer William Dozier, who was keen for an Oriental actor to play the Green Hornet's sidekick Kato. From there his career progressed quickly and Lee found huge fame before his untimely death at the age of 32.

Above: Martial arts exponent Bruce Lee in a karate stance.

YALE COLLEGE
LEARNING RESOURCE CENTRE

Glam Rock

Glam Rock, also known as glitter rock, was an outrageous freak show which hit the big time in 1973 with groups and soloists such as Alice Cooper, Kiss, Slade, Gary Glitter, David Essex, Suzi Quatro, T Rex and David Bowie. Its arrival on the scene couldn't have been better timed with rock reaching its evolutionary peak.

Rock needed to go back to basics after the progressive groups of the late 1960s and early 1970s who thought a song should be an epic 20 minutes. Glam rock gave popular music the get dressed-up, get freaky, get down and get with it approach. Despite the demise of glam rock by 1975, it did set the stage for punk which was to follow.

Although there were some glam rock stars in the US, it was mainly a UK phenomenon where the rhythm of the music was the identifying factor (and not the outfits or make-up). It had a basic 'tribal' 4 beat which could come in many guises, such as Gary Glitter being accompanied by a tom tom or by the whole band stomping their feet, like Slade or T Rex.

It was simple, but effective and completely turned its back on Prog-Rock (those 20 minute epics again), classical music, time changes or augmented chords, concentrating entirely on cartoon rock. It was un-hip to be into glam rock – hence hippies wore loon pants

without feeling like glam kids – and many derided the outrageous the hair styles and over the top make-up. But the three minute outbursts were to form part of the platform for UK punk rock.

Alice Cooper was the only bona-fide US glam rock artist (although Kiss were also popular and only got away with wearing lipstick because they're 'comic

53

Middle: Alice Cooper performing on stage with a boa constrictor.
Above right: Suzi Quatro and her group from l to r, Len Tuckey (guitarist) whom she later married, Keith Hodge (drums) and Alastair McKenzie (keyboards).

1970 1971 1972 1973 1974 1975 1976 1977 1978 1979

book'). Suzi Quatro, a friend of Alice Cooper's, was discovered by Mickie Most who took her away from playing bass in an all girl band in the States, brought her to the UK, put her in leather and created the Queen of Glam Rock.

Chopper bikes

The Raleigh Chopper was the coolest bike on the market and by 1973 had become the UK's best selling bike and is now an icon of the 1970s. Despite the fact that it was fairly ugly, with its back wheel larger than its front, and had a long seat, it was the first designer bike on the market and by 1973 was every boy's dream. With its central gear change and long upright handlebars it was impractical, impossible to ride without falling off and possibly the most unstable bike of all time.

Released in the UK some three or four years earlier, the Chopper followed what had been a rather conservative cycling history in the UK.

Bike designs from the 1930s through to the late-1960s didn't look that different from the early-1970s versions. The film *Easy Rider* released in the UK in 1969, starring Peter Fonda, ensured that bikes moved with the times and the Chopper culture was born. Raleigh saw the opportunity and released the first UK Choppers in September 1969. Cycle dealers in Croydon, Manchester and Newcastle were given 500 bikes in the run up to Christmas that year and demand

Above: The Radiotelephone Chopper Bicycle not mentioned in text!

Spencer – always wearing a beige mac or pyjamas (when at home) – was a wimp who was continually accident-prone and ineffectual despite being extremely well intentioned.

Crawford perfected the character of Spencer and gave him childlike qualities which could have become tedious if it wasn't weren't for the most amazing physical and hysterical comedy seen on television. Crawford performed some amazingly dangerous stunts in the name of comedy including hanging over a cliff edge while hanging onto the exhaust pipe of a Morris Minor and roller skating under a moving lorry to name but two. The plots for each episode were not particularly memorable, but the stunts, daring and sheer entertainment made the show a huge hit. Played by Michele Dotrice, Betty was Spencer's sweet, patient and long-suffering wife who calmly dealt with every chaotic situation that her quirky husband got himself into.

was so huge that the bike made it into January 1970s sales catalogue.

The Chopper was revamped and reintroduced in the twenty-first century but without the trademark gear change.

Some Mothers Do 'Ave 'Em

There were only ever 22 episodes of *Some Mothers Do 'Ave 'Em* starring Michael Crawford as Frank Spencer, but, its enduring popularity is testimony to the fact that sitcom characters can become household names. The character and his antics propelled actor Crawford to superstardom and comic genius.

Above: Stars of Easy Rider on their Chopper bikes.
Below: Portrait of Michael Crawford.

Noel Coward dies

The actor, playwright and composer Noel Coward died from natural causes on 26 March 1973 at the age of 73 from natural causes following severe arthritis and memory loss. He was buried in Firefly Hill, Jamaica where he settled in the late 1950s having left the UK for tax reasons. He was knighted in 1970 for his services to films, theatre and music.

Coward left Paris at the start of the Second World War and took time off from writing to entertain the troops. As well as performing, however, he was engaged by MI5 to conduct intelligence work. Being unable to

reveal details of his work for the Secret Service, he was greatly frustrated by criticism of his opulent life-style while it seemed others around him were suffering.

The 1940s saw some of his best plays including *This Happy Breed* and *Blithe Spirit* which, due to its huge comic success, was later made into a film directed by David Lean due to its huge comic success.

Below: Noel Coward at Buckingham Palace, to receive a Knighthood.

56

witnessed had a profound effect on the Rolling Stones frontman and this month saw the band play a benefit gig at the L.A. Forum to raise money to help the victims.

More than 18,000 fans turned out to see the Stones, Santana and Cheech & Chong, raising $350,000 in the process. In May, Mick and Bianca presented a cheque for $500,000 to the United States Senate in Washington DC, the total having been bolstered by a personal donation of $150,000 from Jagger himself.

In February, the band toured Australia and New Zealand, after projected dates in Japan had been cancelled due to problems gaining work permits. In September, they followed the release of 'Goat's Head Soup' with a lengthy European tour, which proved to be guitarist Mick Taylor's last with the band.

There was a revival in his popularity in the 1960s which led to new productions of some of his 1920s plays.

MUSIC

January

Just days before Christmas 1972, a devastating earthquake destroyed much of Managua, capital of Nicaragua, and birthplace of Mick Jagger's then-wife Bianca. In the wake of the disaster, the Jaggers flew to Managua to find Bianca's family, but the suffering they

February

Early this month, Queen recorded their first radio session, for John Peel's *Top Gear* programme. Although they'd been together for two years, and had already recorded their first album, the band's policy of eschewing live work in favour of honing their playing skills and writing new material meant they were still virtually unknown, so this was an ideal opportunity to raise awareness.

Featuring four songs which would appear on their debut LP in July, the session was broadcast on 15 February, and proved to be the first of six they recorded

Above: British rock group Queen. The band are, from left to right, John Deacon, Freddie Mercury, Roger Taylor and Brian May.

1970 1971 1972 1973 1974 1975 1976 1977 1978 1979

1979 1978 1977 1976 1975 1974 1973 1972 1971 1970

for the Beeb – the last of the six was recorded, 'just for fun', at the height of punk in October 1977, some three years after its predecessor!

Success was far from immediate – a seven-month delay in releasing the album and a badly mismanaged promotional campaign resulted in poor sales and media suspicion. But the band worked tirelessly in the months that followed, and made their breakthrough early the following year.

July

By the time David Bowie's Ziggy Stardust world tour reached Britain, the afraid-of-flying star had sailed the Atlantic on the Queen Elizabeth II, taken the Trans-Siberian Express across Russia and endured nine road-weary months. 'After America, Moscow, Siberia, Japan… I just want to go home to Beckenham and watch the telly,' he told *Melody Maker*. But he had

already decided his fictional creation, the red-haired, androgynous Ziggy Stardust and backing group the Spiders From Mars would stalk the stage no longer: three days into July, on the stage of the Hammersmith Odeon, he'd kill off his creation to the horror of his teenage fans who'd sent new album 'Aladdin Sane' to the top of this month's UK charts.

'Ziggy was created out of arrogance,' he reflected in 1977. 'I was young and I was full of life. But I became obsessed night and day with the character…David Bowie went totally out of the window. Everyone was convincing me I was the Messiah.' In 1973, he probably was…

Above and below: David Bowie in concert at the Hammersmith Odeon, during the last performance he made in the guise of his character Ziggy Stardust.

August

Just three days after the release of his latest album, 'Innervisions', Stevie Wonder suffered serious head injuries and lay in a coma for several days after the car he was travelling in collided with a logging truck near Salisbury, North Carolina. Thankfully, the Motown star made an almost complete recovery, the only lasting legacy of the crash being that he lost his sense of smell. For some time afterwards, however, he would tire easily and suffer headaches, delaying his return to regular live work for over a year.

Wonder, just 23, had the world at his feet when the accident happened – he had re-negotiated his Motown contract, ensuring complete artistic control over future releases and tours, and had produced two of the decade's most accomplished albums in 'Talking Book' (1972) and his latest release. Touring with the Rolling Stones in 1972 had also brought him to the attention of a huge white audience, and hopes for the future were high.

The 1974 Grammy awards saw Wonder nominated in no less than seven categories – he won five, including the most prestigious of all, Album Of The Year, for 'Innervisions'. He also won Best Male R&B Vocal Performance and Best R&B Song (both for 'Superstition'), Best Pop Vocal performance (for 'Sunshine Of My Life') and Best Engineered Non-Classical Recording (again for 'Innervisions'), on the way to a record-breaking lifetime total of 21 Grammy awards.

Almost immediately afterwards Wonder stunned everyone by announcing his intention to retire. He would spend two years touring North America to raise money for charity, undertake a Farewell World Tour at the end of 1975, then move to Africa to work with handicapped children. Happily for his many fans, he was persuaded to carry on as before, raising awareness of the issues close to his heart through his work, which continued to break new ground as the decade progressed.

1970 1971 1972 1973 1974 1975 1976 1977 1978 1979

Below: Stevie Wonder.

1970 1971 1972 1973 1974 1975 1976 1977 1978 1979

Perhaps the best summation of Wonder's mid-70s stature came in 1975, when Paul Simon opened his own Grammy acceptance speech by thanking Stevie for 'not making an album this year'.

September

The opening night of Elton John's sell-out US tour revealed a spectacular stage set featuring a massive staircase, palm trees and five grand pianos, each a different colour, with open lids that spelt out the singer's name. Performing a total of 16 numbers, including the title track of his forthcoming double album 'Goodbye Yellow Brick Road', the artist formerly known as Reginald Dwight was enjoying his most successful period in the US, ushered in by the success of the single 'Crocodile Rock' late in 1972.

For the next three years, he could do no wrong, amassing no less than six Number 1 and three Number 2 singles, while every one of his albums from 'Honky Chateau' (1972) to 'Rock Of The Westies' (1975) topped the charts, staying there for a combined total of 39 weeks.

In the UK, John managed only one Number 1 single during the same period, and even that was

not as a solo artist. 'Don't Go Breaking My Heart', recorded with Kiki Dee, remained his only UK chart-topper until his re-recording of 'Candle In The Wind' swept all previous sales records aside in 1997.

Above and below: The flamboyant Elton John performing in concert in a not very outlandish outfits!

REMEMBER THE SEVENTIES

On the road, Elton John broke not only broke box office and attendance records, he also tried his best to break the bank. He travelled with several wardrobes full of exotic stage clothes, including sequinned jumpsuits, Sgt Pepper-style military outfits, silks, satins, wigs and feathers. He was reputed to have over £25,000 worth of customised glasses, some of them encrusted with jewels, others illuminated, and he wore the most outrageous platform heels on multi-coloured shoes and boots. Rock theatre was at its height in the early-1970s, with Alice Cooper and Genesis leading the way, but an Elton John show was something else – pure spectacle, the ultimate rock'n'roll circus.

SPORT

Jackie Stewart wins third F1 title and retires

Scotsman Jackie Stewart became the first superstar of Formula 1 with his shoulder-length hair and a willingness to talk to the media. He won three World Championships between 1969-73 and has long campaigned to improve safety measures such as introducing full-face helmets, seatbelts and longer run-off areas on dangerous corners.

Born John Young Stewart on 11 June 1939 in Milton, Dumbartonshire, Jackie's first attempts at racing saloons and sports cars brought him to the attention of Ken Tyrrell who invited him to drive for his Formula 3 team in 1963. After winning seven consecutive races, Stewart moved into Formula 1 with BRM after two years and he won his first Grand Prix in Italy the same year.

He left BRM for Tyrrell once they joined the F1 circuit in 1968 and won his first world title the following year, including a triumph in the fog at Germany's Nürburgring where his closest rival was four minutes behind. The team struggled to be competitive in 1970 and Stewart won just

Below: Jackie Stewart.

61

1970 1971 1972 1973 1974 1975 1976 1977 1978 1979

once, in Spain, but they returned the following year with the car to beat. Six more Grand Prix victories ensued as he won his second title but it was the 1973 season that would be most dramatic.

With Fittipaldi and Emerson hot on his heels in the ever-improving Lotus, Stewart – who had decided to retire at the end of the season – had to be at his best and claimed another five wins to propel him to a third crown. The last race, though, at Watkins Glen (America) saw his team-mate François Cévert suffer a fatal accident during Saturday morning qualifying and Stewart withdrew from the race along with the rest of the Tyrrell team.

His 27 Grand Prix victories and three world titles proclaimed him the best since Juan Manuel Fangio. In 1997 he formed his own Stewart Grand Prix team before selling to Ford, who renamed it Jaguar.

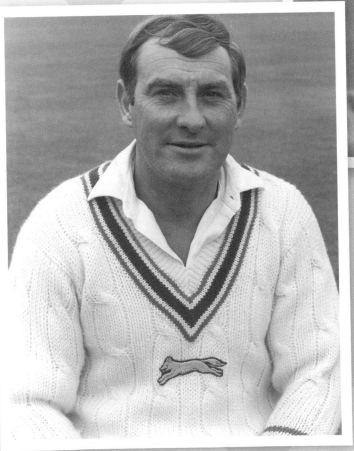

Ray Illingworth sacked as England cricket captain after record defeat

England cricket captain Ray Illingworth found himself removed from the hot seat after 31 Tests (12 wins, 14 draws and five defeats) following an embarrassing defeat against the West Indies in the Wisden Trophy.

Illingworth, born on 8 June 1932, had enjoyed domestic success with Yorkshire and Leicestershire but failed to lead his

Below: Portrait of Ray Illingworth.

Bobby and Jack Charlton play their last game on the same day

The two most famous footballing brothers England has ever seen left their clubs on the same day of the 1972–73 season. On 28 April 1973, Bobby Charlton made the last of his 754 appearances for Manchester United in a 1-0 defeat away to Chelsea while brother Jack announced his retirement as Leeds lost 3-1 at Southampton.

Of course, it was not the first time that the pair had achieved the same thing at the same time: both players were an integral part of England's 1966 World Cup-winning team. Bobby still holds the record for the most goals scored in an England shirt with 49 between 1958-70 and is third in the all-time appearance table with 106, behind Peter Shilton (125) and Bobby Moore (108) while Jack made 35 appearances between 1965-70.

Jack, born in Ashington on 8 May 1935, made his Leeds debut against Doncaster Rovers in April 1953 and went on to make a record 772 appearances and score 95 goals during his time at Elland Road. His medal collection included the League Championship, FA Cup, League Cup and Fairs Cup (twice).

Bobby, born on 11 October 1937 in Ashington, survived United's 1958 Munich air disaster to become an Old Trafford legend and is still the club's record appearance holder. He has also scored more goals than

troops to the victory required to draw the series and the Third Test at Lord's was lost by a record innings and 226 runs.

That wasn't the only embarrassment for England as a packed Lord's saw 28,000 spectators evacuated after a bomb hoax that had to be taken seriously bearing in mind the IRA's activities at the time.

The first Test had been won by the West Indies by a 158-run margin and such was the decline in English cricket that it would be another 27 years before the trophy was once again held aloft by an English captain.

Above: Footballing brothers Bobby and Jack Charlton (right).

1970 1971 1972 1973 1974 1975 1976 1977 1978 1979

anyone else with a total of 247 for the Red Devils. His medal tally at Old Trafford included League Championships (three), FA Cup and European Cup.

They had followed in the footsteps of their four professional footballer uncles along with a cousin, the legendary Newcastle United Number 9 Jackie Milburn.

Both brothers tried their hands at management, with Jack enjoying most success with Middlesbrough and Eire. Bobby, meanwhile, is a director at Manchester United and was knighted in 1994.

POLITICS & CURRENT AFFAIRS

Britain joins the Common Market

On 1 January 1973, the United Kingdom joined the European Economic Community (EEC), widely known at the time as the Common Market. Edward Heath had long been an advocate of joining the community, but Britain had been thwarted in its previous attempts by the veto of Charles de Gaulle. The French president had said he doubted Britain's political will, but it was widely

believed that he secretly feared that English would be adopted as the main language of the Community.

Prior to 1973, the EEC had six members. Now, with Ireland and Denmark also joining, it would have nine. While a thousand UK civil servants prepared to board the gravy train to Brussels, prime minister Heath attempted to persuade everyone that joining the

great cross-fertilisation of knowledge and information, not only in business but in every other sphere. This will enable us to be more efficient and more competitive in gaining more markets, not only in Europe but in the rest of the world.'

Member nations of the British Commonwealth were not wholly convinced by Mr Heath's argument.

There had been no referendum on joining the Common Market, and many people in this country were sceptical. Many still are, especially since the economic union has inevitably become much more of a political union. A referendum on whether or not to remain within the European Economic

community was right for the nation. He spoke as follows:

'It is going to be a gradual development and obviously things are not going to happen overnight. But from the point of view of our everyday lives we will find there is a

Above: Public demonstration against Britain's entry into the Common Market.
Below: The front covers of newspapers reporting Britain's entry into the Common Market.

Community was held by new prime minister Harold Wilson in 1975, but with all the main political parties campaigning in favour of continued membership, the British people were talked into it without too much difficulty.

United States pulls out of Vietnam

American involvement in Vietnam went back many years. At first there was a certain amount of enthusiasm for a 'war against communism' which had been started in 1946, but gradually attitudes changed. More and more American servicemen were being killed and wounded, and the 1960s and early-1970s saw the birth and development of massive world-wide protest against the war. There was a growing feeling that South Vietnam would succumb eventually to President Ho Chi Minh's North Vietnamese forces, and even the mighty Americans would be unable to prevent that happening.

By the late-1960s, it seemed that everyone wanted out of south-east Asia. The death and destruction caused by the war in Vietnam, and in nearby Cambodia,

the conflict. By 1972, US president Richard Nixon was doing his best to extricate his country with some sort of honour, but negotiations were tough and the North Vietnamese were unyielding. Together with others – notably Henry Kissinger, who was to win the Nobel Peace Prize for his efforts – he did however persevere, and he finally announced that the last troops would be

had been seen by millions on film and television the world over, and many returning service personnel were bitter in their condemnation of America's involvement in

withdrawn on 29 March 1973. In an emotional voice he said; 'The day we have all worked and prayed for has finally come.'

Below: A Vietnamese village burning during the Vietnam War.

Phillips of the Queen's Dragoon Guards. Anne and Mark had met through their fondness for all things equestrian. In addition to the flag-waving multitude, some 500 million people world-wide watched the event on television. It was the first time a royal had married a commoner since the future King George VI had married the lady who would one day become the Queen Mother, so it was all very exciting.

Like so many twentieth century royal marriages, this one was doomed to eventual failure. Having produced two children – Peter and Zara – the couple were to divorce in 1992. Both later re-married with rather less splendour, Princess Anne tethering herself to Commander Timothy Laurence shortly after the divorce.

The last United States soldier to be killed in Vietnam, one Lt Col William B Nolde, had met his end just two months before Nixon's announcement. The war was hardly over, but no more Americans would come under fire. Richard Nixon had many problems as president, and his presidential career was to end in ignominy, but he does deserve some credit for getting his fellow citizens out of Vietnam.

Princess Anne Marries

On 14 November 1973 there was a royal wedding at Westminster Abbey. As ever, crowds lined the streets to see the happy couple who, on this occasion, were the Queen's daughter, Princess Anne, and Captain Mark

Above: Princess Anne and her husband Captain Mark Phillips on the balcony of Buckingham Palace after their wedding.
Below: Sergeant Major David Dodd putting the finishing touches to their wedding cake.

1974

FASHION, CULTURE & ENTERTAINMENT

The Rock Festival – Knebworth and Windsor

By 1967, rock festivals were considered the most ideal way for fans to hear rock music. Knebworth country house near Stevenage, 30 miles north of London, was the setting chosen on 20 July 1974. Bands at the show included Van Morrison,

Tim Buckley, The Allman Brothers Band, The Doobie Brothers, The Alex Harvey Band and The Mahavishnu Orchestra. Attracting a crowd of 60,000 it was the first rock festival to be held on the site.

Since festivals began at Knebworth, many high profile bands and artists have performed there including Pink Floyd, The Rolling Stones, Genesis, Frank Zappa, Led Zeppelin, Mike Oldfield, The Beach Boys, Cliff Richard,

Below: Guitarist John McLaughlin playing a double-necked guitar in performance with his band The Mahavishnu Orchestra.

68

three days attracting crowds of more than 350,000 (while a further 3.5 million watched live on television).

Although Knebworth was celebrating its first rock festival in 1974, Windsor Great Park was to hold its third festival in late August that year. Surrounded by controversy due to its proximity to Windsor Castle, the Windsor Free Festival would not go on to enjoy the longevity of other events such as Glastonbury or Reading. Fighting and protests against the police saw 220 people arrested and 50 people (including 22 policemen) injured.

The festival had more than 2,000 attendees camping at the site and more than 600 officers were sent in to move them as festival organisers had not sought permission for people to camp in Windsor Great Park. Festival-goers were unhappy about the police presence and felt that officers were unnecessarily heavy-handed. This resulted in about 400 people marching through Windsor town centre in protest.

Deep Purple, Queen (their last show with the late Freddie Mercury), Paul McCartney, Tears for Fears, Eric Clapton, Dire Straits, Elton John, Robert Plant, Status Quo and Phil Collins. Other performers include The Charlatans, Kula Shaker, The Prodigy, Oasis, Manic Street Preachers, Ocean Colour Scene and Robbie Williams who performed over

1970 1971 1972 1973 1974 1975 1976 1977 1978 1979

Above: Tents in Windsor Great Park during the pop festival.
Below: A hippy enjoying the music and atmosphere at Knebworth rock festival.

REMEMBER THE SEVENTIES

The Wombles

Born in Paris in 1928, Elizabeth Beresford was the daughter of a successful novelist and goddaughter of Walter de la Mare and Eleanor Farjeon. With a home full of books, Elizabeth became an avid reader at a young age.

Beresford started work as a ghost-writer and wrote speeches for the rich and famous before training to be a journalist. She wrote for radio, film and television columns while also working for BBC radio as a reporter. The *Wombles* was inspired by a child on Wimbledon Common she heard pronounce it as Wombledon Common. Within ten years, Beresford had written more than 20 books about the *Wombles* (which were translated into more than 40 languages),

30 TV films and a stage show, a version of which ran in the West End. *Womble* soap, T-shirts, mugs, and soft toys hit the high street and were popular with children nationwide.

The first *Wombles* book published in 1968 was broadcast on the children's story programme *Jackanory*. Soon after, the BBC decided to make the animated series for television. With the motto, 'Make good use of bad rubbish', the *Wombles* were all based on people in Beresford's own life. Great Uncle Bulgaria was modelled on her father-in-law,

Below: Great Uncle Bulgaria from the TV series 'The Wombles'.

creators were the first to recognise its potential. Graphics were displayed on a video screen which immediately reacted to user input. The concept was revolutionary – even a mobile phone in 1970 needed a mainframe computer (which would have been the size of a small apartment) – but by drawing two very small lines (to act as bats) with a line for a net and a square for the 'ball', technology of the early 1970s was able to cope.

Based on the idea of table tennis, Pong consisted of the square travelling across the screen in a linear trajectory. When the square hit the perimeter of the game (outlined by white lines on screen), or one of the 'bats', it ricocheted across the screen with speed and direction being determined by the angle at which it hit the lines

Madame Cholet on her own mother, Tobermory on her brother while Orinoco was based on her son. Other characters were Tomsk, Wellington, Bungo, Alderney, Shansi and Stepney.

With imaginative voices for the animation provided by Bernard Cribbens, puppets by Ivor Wood and music from Mike Batt, the *Wombles*' popularity grew quickly worldwide – Beresford was even known to have enchanted more than a thousand Zulu warriors with *Womble* stories. The *Wombles* even had their own theme tune with the lyric 'Underground, overground, wombling free'. Elizabeth Beresford was awarded the MBE in 1998.

The Atari video game, Pong

Pong, a video game based on ping-pong was the first video game to win widespread popularity. Released by Atari, in both arcade and home console versions, its

originally. Two players moved their bats vertically (the only move on offer at the time) to defend their position with the objective being to bypass the opponent and score points. Another innovation was that it was possible for one player to test their wits against a computerised opponent.

Streakers

On 20 April 1974, 25-year-old Australian Michael O'Brien was the first streaker to bare all at a major event when he ran naked onto the pitch at Twickenham while France and England were playing rugby. Streaking is a non-sexual act that involves taking clothes off and intending to surprise a large group of people.

Cricket is another sport that seems to have had more than its fair share of streakers. It is not uncommon for a streaker to run out onto the field

Above: Australian Michael O'Brien runs nude across the field during the France-England Memorial rugby match at Twickenham, becoming the first streaker at a major sporting event.

purely to shock and entertain by hurdling the stumps and less commonly to make a political statement. Sometimes, streaking can just be a silly drunken prank.

A young bookshop assistant from Petersfield in Hampshire called Erica Roe caused a storm at Twickenham in 1982 when she ran, topless, across the pitch at an England versus Australia rugby match. She found herself escorted away from the game by a policeman covering her breasts with his helmet. Her performance caused a media frenzy and several television interviews for the exhibitionist.

Blazing Saddles

Written by and starring Mel Brooks, *Blazing Saddles*, released in 1974 was the ultimate Western spoof. The non-politically correct comedy is one of Brooks's funniest and most popular films filled with cliches, sexism and toilet humour. Crude and rude, the film contains all the elements of a Western with dance-hall girl, gunslinger, sheriff and good townsfolk. However, everything is turned upside down and the film features a racist town with a black sheriff, played by Clevon Little and Harvey Korman plays a corrupt Hedley Lamarr. Brooks himself plays three cameo roles including the sex-crazed Governor, an indian chief and a First World War aviator.

Brooks wrote lyrics for three songs in the film, which also stars Gene Wilder, Slim Pickens and Madelaine Kahn and Count Basie as himself. Despite only being Brooks's second major film, it was nominated for three Academy Awards including Best Film Editing, Best Song and Best Supporting Actress. It didn't win any awards, but is one of his most successful films.

MUSIC

March

Television and the Ramones, two very different bands who were later acknowledged as being seminal influences on the UK Punk movement of the late 1970s, both made their live debut at New York venues this month. Television, whose music was more art rock than punk rock, played the Townhouse Theatre on the 2 March, while the Ramones took their frantic, minimalist brand of guitar-driven rock to the city's Performance Studio on 30 March.

Both bands soon earned a reputation as impressive live acts, and by August each had secured a residency at one of the top US underground venues – The Ramones at CGBG's in

Below: Mel Brooks (left) sits on the floor beside Harvey Korman as Cleavon Little kneels atop a desk, in a still from the film, 'Blazing Saddles'.

1970 1971 1972 1973 1974 1975 1976 1977 1978 1979

New York, and Television at Max's, Kansas City, where they opened for the Patti Smith Group.

Within a couple of years, there would be a thriving NY underground scene, including Blondie, The Cramps, Richard Hell and the Voidoids, Talking Heads and Suicide, each very different, but each to some degree responsible for inspiring the new generation of angry young men in the UK.

April

The face of Eurovision was changed forever this month, when Abba swept all before them at the Dome, in

73

Above: American punk rock group The Ramones.

Brighton with 'Waterloo'. A world away from the customary Eurovision fare, this was a catchy, confident, pop-rock song with a wickedly infectious chorus. Even the lyrics, simple as they may have been, were a significant improvement over almost everything that had gone before, and more than thirty years later, 'Waterloo' still stands as Eurovision's finest hour.

Perhaps their success stemmed from the fact that Abba represented something new in the 1970s music scene – until now, there had been hard rock, prog rock and the blues for the more serious music fan, while glam rock and throwaway pop songs dominated the charts. Abba were different – a well-crafted product that filled the gap between the two. Catchy, for sure, but the obvious quality of the songs and the production values

set them apart. It was a formula that would bring the group almost unprecedented success across the world over the next few years, including 18 consecutive Top Ten singles and eight chart-topping albums in the UK alone. At one point, Abba were declared Sweden's most successful export after Volvo.

'Waterloo' was actually Abba's second stab at Eurovision success – the group had entered the previous year's contest to find the Swedish entry, coming third with 'Ring, Ring'. Their efforts were possibly hampered by having chosen to call themselves Björn and Benny, Agnetha and Anni-Frid, a fact clearly not lost on the band themselves, since they started looking for an alternative soon afterwards. It was the group's manager, Stig Anderson, who came up with the

Above: Members of ABBA posing at Waterloo railway station in London.

acronym that would come to dominate the late-1970s pop scene.

After Abba ceased to exist in the early-1980s, the various members have had widely differing fortunes – Benny Andersson and Bjorn Ulvaeus continued to work together, taking their music into the theatre with *Chess* and the hugely successful *Mamma Mia!* Agnetha Faltskog embarked on a sporadic solo career, punctuated by periods of inactivity and reports of psychiatric treatment for a number of phobias, including a fear of heights, crowds, flying, driving and open spaces. Anni-Frid Lyngstad initially looked set for solo success, but the failure of her second album prompted her final withdrawal from the music scene in the mid-1980s.

May

Disaster struck during a David Cassidy concert at London's White City stadium this month. 30 fans were taken to hospital, and several hundred more received on-the-spot medical assistance after the hysterical teenage crowd surged forward to get closer to their hero. Cassidy's impassioned pleas for the fans to 'get back' could barely be heard over the commotion, and inevitably went unheeded. One fan, 14-year-old Bernadette Whelan, tragically died of her injuries four days later.

The ill-fated show was the penultimate of a world tour billed as Cassidy's last, the singer having already decided that it was time to reshape his career and try to appeal to a more mature

Above: David Cassidy.
Below: An audience of young pop fans at a David Cassidy concert at White City Stadium.

1970 1971 1972 1973 1974 1975 1976 1977 1978 1979

audience. It was a logical step – Cassidy was now 24, and had already decided to quit *The Partridge Family*, the TV series that had rocketed him to fame four years earlier. Unfortunately, like so many teen idols before and since, he found it all but impossible to re-brand himself, and quietly faded from view as the decade progressed.

October

After 15 months on sale, Mike Oldfield's one-man instrumental masterwork 'Tubular Bells' finally topped the charts, taking over from its follow-up 'Hergest Ridge'. The first release from Richard Branson's Virgin Records label, 'Bells' built a reputation through word of mouth, and its success would force the reclusive guitarist, whose life's work it had been since leaving

Kevin Ayers's employ, to send the music out on tour – even if he got other guitarists – Steve Hillage and, later, a pre-Police Andy Summers – to play the twiddly bits in his stead!

Singer Claire Hamill, later of Wishbone Ash, recalls encountering Oldfield at the Branson-owned Manor studios in Oxford. 'I asked who the weird guy in the corner of the kitchen was, recording during 'down time',' she says, receiving the answer: ''It's Mike.' He played me a tape one night …it was very odd and I didn't understand it. Imagine how I amazed I was when it went to the top of the charts! 'Tubular Bells' is one of those crazy albums that became part of everyone's history.' Oldfield has since re-recorded the album, with John Cleese replacing the late Viv Stanshall as master of ceremonies.

November

Although no-one could have known it at the time, a piece of musical history was made at New York's Madison Square Garden on the 28 November, when John Lennon made what proved to be his final appearance on stage, as the surprise guest at Elton John's Thanksgiving night gig. It was also Lennon's first public appearance for almost two years, and came about as the result of a bet between the two performers.

The story started some months earlier, when Elton collaborated with Lennon on 'Whatever Gets You Thru The Night', a track that later appeared on Lennon's 'Walls And Bridges' album, and which was released as a single to promote it. Lennon wasn't entirely convinced that the song was a winner, but Elton was more

Above: Mike Oldfield, best known for his epic 'Tubular Bells'.

confident, and agreed to play keyboards and sing backup on the song on one condition – if the single made it to the top of the US charts, Lennon would join him on stage at his New York gig later in the year. Despite Lennon's reservations about the song, it topped the chart for a single week in the early summer, and this was the day that Lennon made good on his promise. The pair performed three numbers together – 'Lucy In The Sky With Diamonds', a version of which was Elton's most recent single release, 'Whatever Gets You Through The Night' itself, and another Beatles song, 'I Saw Her Standing There'.

The gig also marked the end of Lennon's infamous 'lost

Lennon were reconciled backstage. From now on, John would settle down, leaving his 'bad boy' image firmly in the past.

May

Mallory Park racecourse, near Leicester, witnessed chaotic scenes during a Radio 1 Fun Day this month, when dozens of hysterical Bay City Rollers fans had to be rescued from a lake after attempting to swim across

weekend', an 18-month separation from wife Yoko Ono that had seen the ex-Beatle indulge in an orgy of drunkenness and bad behaviour that had attracted serious, and deserved, criticism from the world's press. Elton invited Yoko to the gig, and afterwards she and

to the island at its centre to meet their idols. The Rollers, having arrived on the island by helicopter, were being ferried across to the main event site when hundreds of fans decided they simply couldn't wait, and leapt into the water.

Two weeks later, there were similar scenes of uncontrolled adulation when the boys played at London's Hammersmith Odeon, and 60 fans needed medical attention after their Oxford gig the following evening.

For a few months in 1975, the Bay City Rollers were the undeniable Kings of Pop, adored by legions of young, tartan-clad girls, loathed by just about everyone

Above: The Bay City Rollers on the set of their pop television programme 'Shang-A-Lang'.
Below: Fans of The Bay City Rollers.

1970 1971 1972 1973 1974 1975 1976 1977 1978 1979

else who took any interest in music. Their first single, 'Keep On Dancing', had squeezed into the Top Ten over three years earlier, but the ball really started rolling early in 1974, when 'Remember (Sha-La-La)' became their second hit, and the first of nine consecutive single releases to emulate their debut. Two singles made it to the very top of the UK charts, as did two of their four Top Ten albums, and the frenzy that surrounded their every move was quickly dubbed 'Rollermania' by the press. For a while, they even had their own TV show, Shang-A-Lang.

Scenes reminiscent of the Beatles' heyday prompted MP Marcus Lipton to complain that promoters were deliberately engineering the hysteria, but the fans didn't care – for them, the Rollers could do no wrong. By the end of 1976, though, the bubble had burst, and the Bay City Rollers story descended into farce. The band members fell out over money, the press gave the lie to their squeaky-clean image, and years later two rival bands led by former members Les McKeown and Eric Faulkner fought a legal battle over the group's name.

In truth, the Rollers were just another lightweight, well-marketed pop act, but it should be said that the group itself was composed of genuine musicians who played live in concert and on most of their albums.

SPORT

Germany World Cup

For the first time in 28 years, football's World Cup was taking place without any England involvement following their elimination from the qualifiers at the hands of Poland that cost manager Sir Alf Ramsey his job.

The Jules Rimet trophy had been awarded to Brazil on the occasion of their third triumph four years earlier, so a new gold statuette named the FIFA World Cup had been commissioned.

Scotland were the only Home Nation who travelled to Germany but, although they were the only team to avoid defeat in the tournament, they failed to progress past the first group stage. Having won their opening game 2-0 against Zaire, they played out a creditable 0-0 draw with reigning Champions Brazil. Only able to draw 1-1 with Yugoslavia, they unfortunately went out on goal difference…their opponents had put nine past Zaire without reply.

The other change to the competition saw the knockout quarter- and semi-final stages disappear to be replaced by a second group phase with the winners

Below: Goalkeeper Sepp Maier holds the World Cup Trophy aloft, after West Germany's victory in the 1974 World Cup Final.

the world: West Germany's Franz Beckenbauer or the Dutch maestro Johan Cruyff.

It was Cruyff who was brought down in the first minute to earn a penalty and Neeskens gave the Dutch the advantage from the spot. The Germans had yet to touch the ball but they quickly got into their stride and claimed their second world title with goals from Breitner (penalty) and Müller.

Rumble in the Jungle

When Muhammad Ali met George Foreman for the World Heavyweight title on 30 October 1974, he was looking to become only the second boxer after Floyd Patterson (in his 1960 rematch with Ingemar Johansson) to regain the crown.

The fight in Zaire – now the Democratic Republic of Congo – was promoter Don King's first venture and he enlisted both Ali and Foreman with the promise of $5 million apiece.

Ali, born on 17 January 1942, was still on his comeback trail after having been suspended for three and a half years for refusing his draft into the army for the Vietnam War. Foreman, born 10 January 1949, had been Champion since beating Joe Frazier in January 1973 but was not accustomed to going the distance. He had won 37 of his 40 fights by knockout and not one of his last eight contests had gone past the second round.

Realising in the first round that he could not outdo Foreman for strength, Ali used his ability to avoid his

going through to the final and the second-placed teams playing off for third place.

Holland won their three games against Argentina, East Germany and Brazil without conceding a goal while West Germany also registered three wins (Yugoslavia, Sweden and Poland) to top their group. Poland beat Brazil 1-0 to claim third place while the world waited to see who would be crowned king of

Above: Muhammad Ali addressing the press at Kinshasa where he is preparing for his fight against World Champion, George Foreman.

1970 1971 1972 1973 1974 1975 1976 1977 1978 1979

opponent's punches while letting the younger man tire himself out. In a move that confused onlookers, Ali seemed to let Foreman rain punches upon him while taunting him but it was all over in the eighth. Foreman was exhausted and Ali found a superb combo that sent him sprawling on to the canvas and unable to beat the count.

Ali would later become the first boxer to win the Heavyweight title a third time (in September 1978) while in 1994 Foreman became the oldest man ever to

later enjoy so much success. Trained by Ginger McCain and ridden by Brian Fletcher, Red Rum entered the 1974 Grand National determined to retain the crown he had won the previous year in record time and became the first horse since Reynoldstown in 1936 to achieve this feat.

win the world title when, at the age of 45, he knocked out Michael Moorer. Both Foreman and Ali are still good friends and were on stage together to receive an Oscar for the 1996 documentary about the fight, *When We Were Kings*.

Red Rum wins Grand National

Everyone knows the name Red Rum, whether they are an avid horseracing fan or know absolutely nothing about the sport, such was the appeal of the three-time Grand National winner.

Born on 3 May 1965, Red Rum won his first race two years later at Aintree, a course where he would

Red Rum won the Grand National again in 1977 to become the first horse ever to win the prestigious race three times. He died on 18 October 1995 after suffering a stroke and was buried near the winning post at Aintree. A statue stands at the course for all to admire and remember the nation's favourite horse.

POLITICS & CURRENT AFFAIRS

Miners bring down the Government

By October 1973 the coal miners were again unhappy with life. There was another large pay claim on the

Above: Three times Grand National Winner, Red Rum, trains on Southport Sands.

table, and the miners' leaders decided to instituted an overtime ban. Electricity workers also banned overtime, and with conflict in the Middle East causing oil prices to

rocket, Britain was destined for a major energy crisis.

Edward Heath's government was unwilling to meet the miners' demands, and would offer only a 7 per cent wage increase. Another State of Emergency was declared, petrol rationing was planned, and another three-day working week instituted in order to save energy. The lights were going out all over Britain, and the situation was deadlocked. Eventually the miners decided to call an all out strike, while

Heath decided to call a snap general election. He was confident that the electorate would vote in another Conservative administration, and that he would thus have a mandate to sort out the miners once and for all. He told the nation: 'This time the strife has got to stop. It is time for you to speak, with your vote.'

Unfortunately for Edward Heath, the nation was divided on the subject. To the surprise of many, a Labour government was elected, although Harold Wilson did not have an overall majority. In fact Labour polled less votes than the Tories, but they did win 301 seats to the Conservatives' 297. Labour made the miners an offer they couldn't refuse, and the country went back to something approaching normal. The minority government could not last long, and in October there was another general election. It was widely

Above: Edward Heath, the prime minister, leaves Downing Street to hand in his resignation to the Queen following defeat for the Conservatives.
Below: Harold Wilson outside 10 Downing Street, at the head of a minority Labour government.

1970 1971 1972 1973 1974 1975 1976 1977 1978 1979

predicted that the Labour Party would this time win a fairly substantial overall majority, but in fact it was another close vote. Wilson did however get an overall majority of three seats, and had no choice other than to make it work.

IRA bombs English pubs

By the early 1970s, the IRA's bombing campaign on the British mainland was well and truly underway, and 1974 saw some of the worst of the atrocities. On Saturday 5 October two pubs were bombed in Guildford, Surrey, which is close to a number of military establishments, were bombed. Five people were to lose their lives, and

recently returned from a tour of duty in Northern Ireland, and many of the injured were also service personnel. Most of the serious casualties were in the Horse and Groom, which had its frontage destroyed by the explosion.

David Howell, a former Minister for Northern Ireland, said at the time:

'I'm afraid I thought I'd seen the last of this in Belfast. It's quite clear that we must hunt down the maniacs and the animals who would do this kind of thing.'

The hunt was indeed on, but a few weeks later two more pub bombs caused yet more loss of life.

a further 65 were injured. The first bomb was detonated at 10.30 p.m. in the Horse and Groom, and the second went off just before closing time in the nearby Seven Stars. Four of the five dead were soldiers who had

In the centre of Birmingham, first the Mulberry Bush and then, a few seconds later, the Tavern in the Town were hit, killing a total of 21 people and injuring around 180. The Mulberry Bush was on the ground floor of a

Below: The aftermath of an IRA bomb at the Horse and Groom pub in Guildford, Surrey.

17-storey office block, while the Tavern in the Town was an underground bar some 45 metres away, used mainly by teenagers.

National Committee, had caused a minor stir in 1972, but few then believed that the US President could have been directly involved in political espionage. However,

There were to be many more IRA bombs during the 1970s (and indeed the 1980s) including one at the home of prime minister Edward Heath in December 1974, and the one that killed Lord Mountbatten in his boat off the Irish coast in 1979.

Nixon resigns

The United States had its fair share of scandals and political mishaps during the twentieth century, but the greatest of all was the Watergate affair. Burglaries at the Watergate Building, the headquarters of the Democratic

as the story unfolded, it became clear that President Nixon was certainly involved in a cover-up.

'Tricky Dicky' got himself into all sorts of trouble with denials, edited tapes, plain old-fashioned lies, and a good deal of swearing. In the end, he was threatened with impeachment – enforced removal from office – and so, on 8 August 1974, he announced on television that he was resigning the presidency. His successor, Gerald Ford, later granted him a pardon, thus ensuring that the former president would not face prosecution, but Nixon maintained his innocence until his dying day.

Above: Richard Nixon with his family after his resignation as President, 1974.

1970 1971 1972 1973 1974 1975 1976 1977 1978 1979

1975

FASHION, CULTURE & ENTERTAINMENT

Charlie Chaplin receives Knighthood

On 4 March 1975, Charlie Chaplin was knighted by the Queen. Recognised for his popular Little Tramp character, complete with moustache, bowler, cane and funny walk, Charles Spencer Chaplin was born on 16 April 1889 in London. He was one of the most prolific actors of early Hollywood.

His talents came from both parents who were musical hall performers, although his father died when he was only 10 and his mother was prone to severe bouts of mental illness – his first stage performance at the age of five was prompted by his mother's illness. Aged eight, he toured in the musical *The Eight Lancaster Lads* and at 10 performed at the London Hippodrome in *Giddy Ostende*. Between the ages of 17 and 24 he toured with the Fred Karno troupe (Stan Laurel was his understudy) and he headed off to New York in 1910. By 1913, Chaplin had secured a contract with Mack Sennett at Keystone – he left for Hollywood a month later.

Chaplin's first movie, *Making A Living* in 1914 was also the first of the 35 films he made that year. The next two years saw Chaplin with Essanay and Mutual

where he went on to make another 26 films. In 1918 he joined First National (later to become part of Warner Brothers) and formed United Artists (UA) with Douglas Fairbanks, Mary Pickford and DW Griffith the following year.

1921 saw Chaplin make his first full-length movie, *The Kid*. 1923's *A Woman Of Paris* was Chaplin's first film for United Artists which he produced and directed himself. At the first Academy

Above: Charlie Chaplin with his wife Oona after receiving a Knighthood at Buckingham Palace.

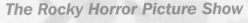

Awards ceremony he won a special award for *The Circus* (1928) for his genius in writing, acting, directing and producing.

In 1943, Chaplin (54) married his fourth wife, Oona O'Neill who was only 17 – the couple were to have three sons and five daughters. Chaplin had 11 children in all. He left the US for Switzerland in 1952 and only returned briefly to receive a special Academy Award honouring his lifetime achievements. Chaplin died aged 88 on Christmas Day 1977 at his estate in Vevey, Switzerland.

The Rocky Horror Picture Show

Based on the original London stage production (1973), *The Rocky Horror Picture Show* was first released in the UK on 14 August 1975. The stage show in the US, starring Meat Loaf, also hit Broadway in 1975, but the film was much more successful than the live performances.

Directed by Jim Sharman and Richard O'Brien, who also wrote the songs, the film became a cult movie. Film-goers today are likely to wear outfits like the characters from the show and behave outrageously throwing food, yelling, dancing and cheering.

The film, a comedy-horror musical, stars Susan Sarandon, Tim Curry (who was also in the original London stage show) and Barry Bostwick. Other actors in both the stage and film version include Richard O'Brien, Patricia Quinn, Nell Campbell and Jonathan Adams. Meat Loaf also makes an appearance for one song while Christopher Biggins can be seen in the chorus.

Straight-laced couple, Brad Majors and Janet Weiss (Bostwick and Sarandon), pledge their engagement after their friends' wedding and decide to visit their mentor and the man that introduced them, Dr Scott (Adams). On the way, their car gets a flat tyre (the spare is also flat) and they end up walking to a remote castle in the woods in search of a telephone.

The castle is a strange place where gender-bending scientist Dr Frank N Furter (Curry) is throwing a party to celebrate the creation of Rocky. Stripped to

Below: Charlie Chaplin performing in 'The Kid'.

their underwear, Frank N Furter shows interest in both Brad and Janet which forces the couple to question their love and loyalty for each other while Rocky becomes more interested in Janet, much to the Doctor's dismay.

Dr Scott's nephew Eddie is being held in the castle by Dr Frank N Furter who used the motorcycling-rocker/delivery boy to provide Rocky's brain. Eddie is murdered and Dr Scott turns up looking for his missing nephew. Dinner is served and Frank N Furter admits that Eddie 'is dinner'. After a chase all characters are turned to stone by Frank N Furter who prepares a floor show before the statues are released. Each character then launches into song about their happiness and experiences. Servant at the castle, Riff Raff (O'Brien) kills both Rocky and Dr Frank N Furter and the others are released from the spell.

Charlie, Brut and Old Spice

1975 was shaping up to be a best-smelling year. Revlon launched Charlie while Henry Cooper and Kevin Keegan advertised Brut and a surfer with a classical soundtrack persuaded men that Old Spice was a best seller and other men splashed on the Denim whose slogan read 'For men who don't have to try too hard.'

First created by Revlon in 1973, Charlie was the definitive perfume for every girl. Worn during the daytime, the fragrance included a mix of citrus, peach and jasmine combined with rose, lily of the valley and carnation. The base of the perfume was made from cedar wood, oak moss and vanilla.

Advertised by sporting heroes Cooper and Keegan, Brut sported the slogan 'Splash it all over' and the vast majority of the nation's men did just that. Brut had a strong, distinctive masculine smell and at the time it

Above: Tim Curry, as Doctor Frank N Furter, reclines in a chair surrounded by (left to right) Nell Campbell, Patricia Quinn and Richard O'Brien in 'The Rocky Horror Picture Show'.

was launched was the first men's fragrance to be quite so bold. Produced by Fabergé, Brut is still sold worldwide today.

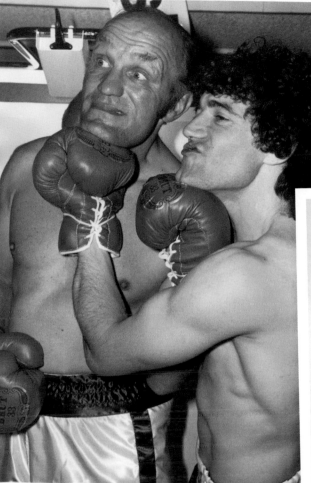

While Brut boys were splashing it all over, Old Spice wearers came riding on the crest of a wave hoping for the best beach babe around to notice them.

8-track

Thought of as revolutionary in the 1960s, the 8-track was designed to change the way that music was listened to. As it transpired, the chunky machine was useless and its popularity relatively short-lived. An 8-track can be either a cartridge – an audio storage magnetic tape – or a reel to reel tape used in professional recording studios allowing the sound engineer to decide which track on the device will be used for each instrument.

The chunky machine version was designed for cars as a stereo which played ¼ inch tapes. Originally designed by Bill Lear in 1964 (inspired by the 4-track stereo tape cartridge system), the 8-track grew alongside the booming car industry. By 1967 8-tracks were a standard feature in many cars and were slowly being introduced to homes. However, by the mid-1970s its popularity waned in the UK and it lost out to the

audio cassette (less than half the size of an 8-track cartridge). Although the 8-track was around until the mid-1980s if you searched hard enough, the arrival of another new format – the CD – made sure its days were numbered permanently.

Above: Henry Cooper and Kevin Keegan promoting the men's aftershave lotion 'Brut'.
Below: 8 track cassette players.

1970 1971 1972 1973 1974 1975 1976 1977 1978 1979

REMEMBER THE SEVENTIES

Hairstyles and Perms

The way we wear our hair has been an all-consuming passion of human nature since time began. From Samson, the Biblical character who lost his strength when his hair was cut to the radical student movements of the 1970s hair has been significant throughout history.

From earliest times people have worn their hair in a variety of ways for many different reasons, be it religion, class or social status. First Lady Jackie Kennedy, along with the stars of Hollywood, popularised the bouffant hairstyle in the 1960s, but by the 1970s the hairstyle became a symbol of a bygone era and few people seemed to notice that it had almost vanished.

But from the late 1960s to early 1970s and the introduction of the counter-culture young people began to question society's values. Both men and women, especially those advocating peace, began to wear their hair long. Hal Ashby's 1975 film, *Shampoo*, is a spoof on celebrity hair stylists while British men rushed to have perms after footballer Kevin Keegan sported the look.

MUSIC

May

The final days of May saw the last performance of one of the most ambitious rock shows ever staged, when Genesis brought their mammoth Lamb Lies Down On Broadway world tour to its conclusion in Paris. It would also be singer Peter Gabriel's final appearance with the band, although the official announcement of his leaving would not follow until August.

'The Lamb Lies Down On Broadway' is still regarded as a high point of progressive rock, but bringing the concept to fruition had not been easy, and the process had torn the band apart. Gabriel had insisted on total control over the storyline and the song lyrics, causing

Above: Kevin Keegan and his mullet!
Below: Phil Collins, drummer and singer with Genesis, takes a break behind his drumkit.

friction within the group, and his absence from many of the album's writing and rehearsal sessions, although due to his wife's difficult pregnancy, further aggravated matters.

The last big story of what proved to be a busy month for music news came on its final day, as the Rolling Stones announced their forthcoming US tour by playing 'Brown Sugar' from the back of a truck moving slowly through New York's Greenwich Village. Not only that, but there would be a new Face on stage with the band – Faces guitarist Ron Wood was to join the Stones as a guest musician on the forthcoming tour, standing in for Mick Taylor who had left the band some months earlier.

Wood's arrival in the Stones camp was a long, drawn-out affair that began in the spring, when he went to Munich to contribute to the band's latest album, 'Black And Blue'. Although still officially with the Faces, the guitarist then played on the US tour before rejoining Rod Stewart and the boys for dates in the autumn, but by December the Faces were no more – Stewart quit, complaining that Wood was 'on permanent loan to the Stones' – and he was free to complete the transfer.

Many predicted the demise of Genesis after Gabriel's departure, but with Phil Collins taking over vocal duties, and a change to a simpler style, the band continued to grow in popularity throughout the decade. Gabriel, meanwhile, went from strength to strength as a solo performer, incorporating world music into his work and latterly branching out into multi-media projects.

Above: Genesis pose at Bitter End Café.
Below: Ron Wood of The Rolling Stones.

1970 1971 1972 1973 1974 1975 1976 1977 1978 1979

October

Two happy events in as many days left John Lennon on top of the world at the beginning of October 1975. After a three-year battle to remain in the US, Lennon was finally given the news that the Court of Appeal had overturned his deportation order, and he would be allowed to stay. The decision to expel him from the US was ostensibly for a UK drugs conviction dating from 1968, but no-one was in any doubt that this was just an excuse, and his political activities during 1971 and 1972 had been the catalyst. The following July, Lennon was finally granted his Green Card, the document confirming his right to stay in the US.

Two days later, on Lennon's thirty-fifth birthday, Yoko Ono gave birth to a healthy baby boy, Sean, and John's happiness was complete. He would shortly announce his retirement from making music, taking time out to be the father to Sean that he'd never managed to be to his earlier son, Julian.

In a bizarre postscript in 2005, newly-released FBI papers revealed that Lennon had eventually been dismissed as a threat to the US because 'he was always stoned'!

November

This month saw the recording of what is arguably the most influential promotional film of all time, when Queen spent just four hours at Elstree Studios putting together a clip to accompany their new single 'Bohemian Rhapsody' on *Top Of The Pops*. The original idea of the clip was simply to allow the group to be seen on the show, even though they were away on tour,

Above: One of John Lennon's peace messages reading 'War Is Over!' that may have contributed to his need to fight to stay in the US.

when considering the routine that might have accompanied such operatics! Following the success of 'Bohemiain Rhapsody', it became par for the course for record companies to produce promo videos for their artists' singles, allowing greater control over presentation, and removing the need for artists to appear in person.

The film was directed by Bruce Gowers, whose earlier work included TV series with Kenny Everett and Larry Grayson. 'Bohemian Rhapsody' was his first music video – taking ideas from the group members, who asked him to bring the cover of their second album to life, it cost just £4,500 to produce using an outside broadcast truck owned by one of the band's managers. Incredibly, all the special effects were done during the recording – the effect of having the face zooming away was achieved by pointing the camera at a monitor, producing visual feedback. Gowers has since gone on to produce countless other music videos, live music shows and MTV awards shows.

Starting at the end of the month, 'Bohemian Rhapsody' spent nine straight weeks at Number 1 in the UK, the first single to do so for 18 years. Just two years later, the BPI named it 'Best Single Of The Last 25 Years', and in December 1991, following Freddie Mercury's death, it topped the British charts once more, becoming the only UK single ever to sell a million copies on two separate occasions.

but it proved to be a turning point in the way music was marketed, and for some time it remained a benchmark for the genre.

It's hard to believe there was ever a time before the pop video, but prior to Queen's groundbreaking effort, if the artist was unavailable, *Top of the Pops* would generally show dancers such as Pan's People performing a routine to the song – the mind boggles

Above: Pan's People, the resident dance troupe from 'Top of the Pops', in action.

1970 1971 1972 1973 1974 1975 1976 1977 1978 1979

SPORT

First Cricket World Cup

The first ever cricket World Cup took place between 7-25 June 1975 and was hosted by England. Only eight nations took part (by 2007 the number will have increased to a record 16) and they were divided into two groups of four for the preliminary matches with the top two going through to the semi-finals.

With 120 overs to get through in a day, the matches started early and the opening day's play saw victories for New Zealand (over East Africa by 181 runs), England (India by 202 runs), Australia (Pakistan by 73 runs) and the West Indies (Sri Lanka by nine wickets).

The second phase of matches didn't throw up any surprise results, but the West Indies suffered a scare and it took a last wicket partnership by Deryk Murray and Andy Roberts to score 64 runs in the last 14 overs to give them a single wicket victory over Sri Lanka.

With a seven-wicket victory over Australia in the final phase, the West Indies went through to the semi-final as group winners to meet New Zealand, runners-up in Group A. The other semi-final paired England with Australia.

Australia claimed victory by four wickets as England set their lowest run score of the tournament with a paltry 93 from 36.2 overs while the West Indies overcame New Zealand by five wickets as they reached their target of 159 in just 40.1 overs.

In the Final, the West Indies batted first and were 50-3 when captain Clive Lloyd stepped up to the

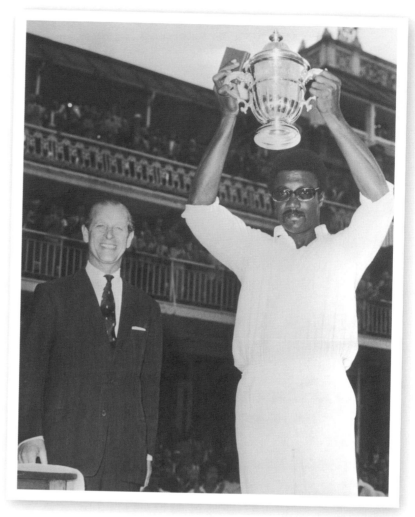

crease. He led from the front-scoring 102 off 85 balls to help his side to a 291-8 total at the end of their 60 overs. Australia put up a brave fight but were all out for 274, with Keith Boyce taking four wickets as the West Indies lifted the Prudential World Cup.

New Zealander John Walker becomes first man to do sub-3.50 mile

On 12 August 1975, New Zealand middle distance runner John Walker became the first man to run a sub-3.50 minute mile when he set a new world record of 3 minutes 49.4 seconds in Gothenburg.

Walker, born on 12 January 1952, was a major force in middle distance running for much of the 1970s

Above: Prince Philip looks on as West Indies captain Clive Lloyd raises the trophy after his team won the final of the Prudential World Cup against Australia, June 1975.

with the highlight of his career being an Olympic gold medal in the 1,500 metres at Montreal in 1976. He also won two Commonwealth Games medals in Christchurch in 1974: silver for the 1,500 metres (he was again placed second at Brisbane in 1982) and bronze for the 800 metres.

Walker retired in 1990 after becoming the first person to run more than 100 sub-four minute miles (129 in total) and was awarded the International Olympic Committee Bronze Order six years later. The same year, the likeable Kiwi was diagnosed with the debilitating Parkinson's Disease.

Barry Sheene crashes at Daytona

British racer Barry Sheene suffered the first of two career-threatening crashes in March 1975 while practicing for the Daytona 200 in Florida. Held annually at the Daytona International Speedway in Daytona Beach, the Daytona 200 is a 68-lap race around the 2.5 mile course.

Sheene suffered a blowout of the rear tyre on his three-cylinder Suzuki during a practice run and crashed at 175 mph, smashing his thigh and breaking his wrist, collarbone and several ribs. Yet, amazingly, he was racing again just five weeks later.

Above: John Walker of New Zealand (black jersey) runs with a pack of racers capturing the gold medal in the men's 1500m event at the 1976 Summer Olympic Games.

Sheene, born on 11 September 1950, received his first bike – a 50cc Ducati – when he was just five. It was given to him by his father, a mechanic who enjoyed racing himself. He won the British 125cc Championship in 1970 before graduating to 500cc bikes.

He won his first World Championship in 1976 on a works Suzuki having claimed victory in five Grands Prix and retained his title the following year with six more chequered flags. Sheene was awarded the MBE in 1978.

His second serious crash came during practice for the British Grand Prix at Silverstone in 1982 when he came over a hill to find an accident in his path and was unable to avoid the wreckage. This time, his legs were in such a state that surgeons spent eight hours realigning his bones and inserted metal pins, plates and screws to keep everything in place.

Sheene retired two years later and emigrated to Australia where the warmer climate helped reduce the aches and pains in his battered body. He was diagnosed with cancer of the stomach and oesophagus in July 2002 and died on 10 March 2003.

After his death, his widow Stephanie agreed that the bikes he won his world titles on could be returned to England and they are currently on display at the National Motor Museum at Beaulieu.

Above: Barry Sheene in action.
Below: Portrait of Barry Sheene, in more pensive mood.

POLITICS & CURRENT AFFAIRS

Inflation reaches 25%

Almost as soon as he was returned to power in 1974, Harold Wilson had trouble with the unions. In fact, he had a great deal of trouble all round, but the unions were a particular problem as they largely funded the

WE CAN'T AFFORD ANOTHER TORY GOVERNMENT.

BEEF
Jone's
First Choice
Thick Sausages
USUAL PRICE
~~17p~~
TORY PRICE 26p

Only Labour can get us out of this mess.

Labour Party. Union leaders were submitting ever bigger wage demands, and with the nationalised industries having weak management structures and poor negotiators, the unions nearly always got more or less what they demanded. Wilson, and his Chancellor of the Exchequer Denis Healey, wanted to avoid a statutory pay policy and hoped to persuade the unions to show

restraint when it came to pay claims. There was a 'social contract' of sorts, but people such as Hugh Scanlon, of the Amalgamated Union of Engineering Workers, said that union leaders like himself would not go along with anything which cut their members' standard of living.

It was all very difficult, especially as there was a good deal of dissent within the ranks of the Labour Party (surprise, surprise!). Industry Secretary Tony Benn was at odds with his leader over just about everything: he once sent Wilson a memo, which led the PM to

Above left and right: A Labour election poster, and Denis Healey, the Chancellor of the Exchequer.

1970 1971 1972 1973 1974 1975 1976 1977 1978 1979

*1970 1971 1972 1973 1974 **1975** 1976 1977 1978 1979*

remark that he hadn't read it, and didn't propose to, but he disagreed with it anyway.

With enormous trade and government deficits, and with wages spiralling out of control, inflation finally hit 25% per cent per annum during 1975. The USA, which had economic troubles of its own, showed concern, and Henry Kissinger is known to have remarked to the new Conservative leader, one Margaret Thatcher: 'Britain is a tragedy.' In 1976, the International Monetary Fund was asked to help Britain out, on the basis that economic progress was being made: Denis Healey claiming that his social contract with the unions had reduced the average increase in earnings from 27.6% to 13.9%. It was a start, but things were actually to become a lot worse during the next few years.

Apollo-Soyuz link-up

Since the Soviet Union had launched its first Sputnik in 1957, there had been intense rivalry between it and the United States regarding the exploration of space. The Americans had not been happy when the Soviets put

the first man in space in 1961, and the Soviets had been equally unhappy when America put the first men on the Moon in 1969. However, by the mid-1970s a spirit of co-operation prevailed. Well, it more or less prevailed.

Midway through 1975, the first real manifestation of this spirit of co-operation occurred. On 15 July a Soviet Soyuz spacecraft, and an American Apollo spacecraft, were launched within a few hours of each other. The idea was that they should link-up, or dock, a couple of days later. This they duly did, and before long the two mission commanders, Tom Stafford and Alexei Leonov, shook hands through the hatch of the Soyuz. It had been calculated that the historic handshake would, somewhat remarkably, take place over Bognor Regis,

Above: American and Russian stamps commemorating a joint US-USSR space mission.

1970 1971 1972 1973 1974 1975 1976 1977 1978 1979

but there was a small cock-up in the calculations, and it actually took place over France.

The two craft remained locked in their metallic embrace for 44 hours, during which time the crews – three Americans and two Russians – exchanged gifts, wandered in and out of each other's spacecraft, signed things, ate meals together, and generally had a jolly time. They also conducted the odd scientific experiment, and practised more docking and re-docking.

At last it was time to say goodbye, and the spacecraft separated for the last time. The Apollo crew made an error during preparations for the return to Earth, which resulted in a difficult and very bumpy landing, and the capsule filling up with poisonous fumes. They got away with it,

however, and no serious damage was done. The Apollo-Soyuz Test Project was regarded as both a scientific and public relations success.

Moorgate tube crash

London's worst ever underground railway disaster occurred on 28 February 1975. During the morning rush hour, a train travelling from Drayton Park to Moorgate Station crashed into a brick wall at 30 mph, just beyond the platform at Moorgate. The train had showed no sign of slowing down as it approached the station, and the cause of the accident remains a mystery. The 55-year-old driver, who died instantly, was not under the influence of drink or drugs, and was not thought to have been likely to want to take his own life. The train had no mechanical defects.

43 people died as a result of the accident, and many more were injured. Rescuers worked in fierce heat to bring the dead and injured out of the wreckage of the first three carriages, which had been crushed together. The last survivor was brought to the surface at 10 p.m.

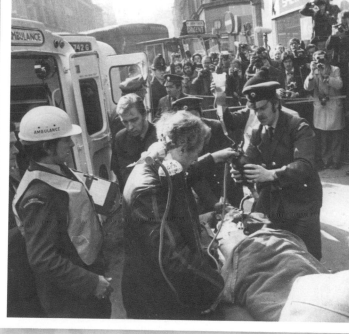

Above: The Soviet Soyuz spacecraft prepares to dock with the American Apollo craft whilst in orbit.
Below: Emergency services help injured passengers at Moorgate Tube station after the train crash.

1976

FASHION, CULTURE & ENTERTAINMENT

Punk

In the mid-1970s, London became the centre for an anarchic and aggressive movement called punk, while a musical style (of the same name)

developed alongside this anti-fashion, urban youth street culture. Clothes from charity shops were cut up and reconstructed to make garments that would attract attention.

Torn fabrics, frayed edges and defaced prints shocked those not involved in the movement, purely because nothing like it had ever been seen before. Punk clothes reflected the lifestyle of those

with little cash due to unemployment and the generally low incomes that were offered to school leavers and students. It became the norm to deliberately tear trousers and reveal

Above: A girl wearing punk clothes and make up, including the words 'No Future' across her forehead.
Below: A punk rock fan attending a concert by the Clash.

conventional attitude. Like platform shoes, the style was unisex and men began to wear facial jewellery.

Punk rock established itself in the mid-1970s as anti-establishment music through bands such as the Ramones, the Sex Pistols, the Damned and the Clash. Often, punk bands emulated US garage rock (popular in the 1960s) and kept to simple musical structures where short songs of around two and a half minutes in length were usual. Fast tempos were common, especially in hardcore punk. Influences from other genres including reggae, rockabilly and funk were common in early punk music.

Ultimately, punk style – tears, safety pins, spiked hair, cut-up newspaper graphics – would prove longer-lasting than the music which went hand in hand with it.

laddered tights worn with Doc Marten's boots while safety pins and chains held clothes together.

Another revolutionary step was the art of body piercing where studs and pins in eyebrows, lips and other body parts were all part of the look. Tattoos and body piercing were designed to offend those with a more

Above: The Sex Pistols.
Below: Joe Strummer (left) and Paul Simonon of the Clash.

1970 1971 1972 1973 1974 1975 1976 1977 1978 1979

Agatha Christie dies

On 12 January 1976, Dame Agatha Christie died at her home in Wallingford, Oxfordshire, aged 85. As the world's most popular novelist, having sold an estimated 300 million books during her lifetime, there were rumours on her death that she had left a multi-million pound fortune. But in fact, when her will was published in April it revealed she had only £106,683. At the time of her death a novel *Sleeping Murder* involving one of her most famous characters, Miss Marple, remained unpublished.

During her lifetime Agatha Christie published 83 novels and established her reputation as a crime writer when she introduced the famous character of Hercule Poirot in *The Mysterious Affair At Styles* in 1920. Having married Colonel Christie in 1914, she was to create her own mystery when she disappeared in 1926 and her car was found abandoned in a chalk pit on the Surrey Downs. She had in fact had a row with her husband and booked into a hotel in Harrogate under the name of her husband's mistress. Eventually Christie divorced and married archaeologist Sir Max Mallowan.

Her disputed income during the late 1950s was estimated at £100,000 a year, but she was a shrewd businesswoman and was careful not to leave her fortune for the taxman. Her hugely successful play, *The Mousetrap* was first written as a radio sketch called *Three Blind Mice* in celebration of Queen Mary's 80th eightieth birthday. It is said to have reportedly made £3 million which Christie gave to her only grandson Matthew Prichard. In 1955 the company Agatha Christie Ltd was formed which was run by Pritchard. Most of her property was left to Max Mallowan and her daughter, Rosalind Hicks. She was made a Dame in 1971.

Saturday morning TV

In 1976, *Multi-Coloured Swap Shop* became a rival to Chris Tarrant's *Tiswas* which had ruled Saturday morning UK television ratings for two years. Hosted by DJs Noel Edmonds with

Below: Dame Agatha Christie.

sidekick Keith Chegwin, the programme was designed as a vehicle for kids to swap literally anything. *Swap Shop* first aired on 2 October 1976 where the first Swaporama, hosted by 'Cheggers' at Cardiff Arms Park attracted 200 children with something to swap. Eventually this element of the show was to attract more than 2,000 participants. The show was entirely live apart from some recorded music sequences and a weekly half hour cartoon slot.

Tiswas (Today Is Saturday, Wear A Smile), hosted by Tarrant, was anarchic in comparison to *Swap Shop*. It attracted a wide audience, probably all eager to see a studio of grown adults throwing custard pies and buckets of water over each other. At best, it was shambolic, subversive and reeked of chaos from start to finish.

The National Theatre opens in London

On 25 October 1976, some 25 years after the Queen first laid a foundation stone on its planned site next to the Festival Hall, the National Theatre finally opened its doors. Designed by Sir Denys Lasdun, the building comprised three theatres. The Olivier and Lyttleton theatres were opened at the official opening by the Queen while the third, the Cottesloe, was opened the following year. To mark the auspicious occasion – and perhaps to make light of years of delays – bands, an outdoor carnival and fireworks entertained the large crowd that had gathered despite pouring rain.

Despite the original stone being laid in 1951, building work did not begin until 1969 due to funding problems. When finally the complex was expected to

Above: The National Theatre on the South Bank.

open in 1973, it was further plagued by delays, but this time because of construction issues. After unveiling a commemorative plaque when it finally did open, the Queen was then treated to a performance of the comedy *Il Campiello* by Goldini. Sir Laurence Olivier was one of the theatre's first directors. It had been previously based at the Old Vic in south-east London.

The Muppets

Muppet creator Jim Henson was keen to launch his own TV series following the success of *Sesame Street*. With regulars, Kermit the Frog (who hosted the show), hot-headed Miss Piggy (in love with Kermit), Fozzie Bear, Gonzo, Scooter, Beauregard, Rowlf and the Electric Mayhem, the show, after

several false starts, became one of the most well-loved comic masterpieces of all time. Each show featured a celebrity guest who was usually ridiculed by various Muppet characters but who shone through the mayhem and madness and taught the Muppets about values and life.

The show lasted for five years and clocked up 120 episodes, several films and two spin-offs. Moulded in the style of the old

Below: Kermit and Miss Piggy.

as the band began to prepare for life after Peter Gabriel. There had been much speculation that Gabriel's departure would spell the end for the arch-progsters, and at this stage most thought their chances of survival were poor. How wrong they were…

In March, to coincide with the release of their first post-Gabriel album 'A Trick Of The Tail', Genesis set out on a North American tour, then in June, they opened their European tour with five nights at the Hammersmith Odeon. Inevitably, the shows were less theatrical than before, but Collins proved a more than adequate replacement for Gabriel, and the new album sold strongly. In the years to come, Genesis would all but abandon their progressive rock roots, adopting a simpler style and becoming a top-selling act across the globe.

This was to be the year of Peter Frampton, ex-guitarist and singer with the Herd and Humble Pie and a double concert album released this month was to be not only the success of 1976 but his entire solo career. 'Frampton Comes Alive' even got a name check in *Wayne's World 2* when Mike Myers, as the eponymous star, said: 'Everybody in the world has 'Frampton Comes Alive'…if you lived in the suburbs you were issued with it. It came in the mail with samples of Tide.'

His first three solo albums sold in the 40,000–70,000 range, the latter actually making the US album Top 30. But the breakthrough came with 1975's 'Frampton' on which he debuted his trademark Talkbox guitar effect, an initial 350,000 sale evidence of growing support. With the success of 'Comes Alive',

music hall, it was a weekly vaudeville show which attracted celebrities such as Bob Dylan, Roger Moore and John Cleese, while popular sketches included 'Pigs in Space' and 'Veterinarians Hospital'.

MUSIC

January

The 'new-look' Genesis, with Phil Collins as lead vocalist and new drummer Bill Bruford, was unveiled this month,

Above: British rock group Humble Pie. From left to right; Peter Frampton, Jerry Shirley, Gregg Ridley and Steve Marriott.

1970 1971 1972 1973 1974 1975 1976 1977 1978 1979

Peter went from a supporting act who could headline only in certain cities – New York, Detroit and San Francisco – to a nationally-known name.

But there was a down side. 'I was happy on one hand, scared shitless on the other hand. It was a huge weight on my shoulders. I had to compete with myself. I went through the ceiling and found myself all alone.' Unfortunately, the double blow of a serious car crash in June 1978, in which he broke an arm and cracked his ribs, plus the following month's critical pasting of the disastrous *Sergeant Pepper's Lonely Hearts Club Band* film in which he starred as Billy Shears saw him drop out of the limelight. But he still tours today, albeit without the shoulder-length tresses that were his visual trademark.

For most bands, being thrown off a tour after just one night might have been a major set-back, but for the Sex Pistols it proved to be the start of something big... The Pistols managed just one night of this month's Eddie & the Hot Rods tour, an explosive appearance at London's Marquee club, during which fights broke out and furniture was hurled across the auditorium. Beneath the year's most prophetic headline – *'Don't look over your shoulder but the Sex Pistols are coming'* – Neil Spencer described the band as playing '60s-style white punk rock',and a new musical genre was born. In the same article, guitarist Steve Jones

summed up the band's ethos – 'Actually, we're not into music, we're into chaos.'

By April, the band were playing regularly at the El Paradiso Club in Soho, and Johnny Rotten was setting out his rock manifesto – 'I hate hippies and what they stand for. I hate long hair. I hate pub bands... I want people to see us and start something, or else I'm just wasting my time.'

As the summer progressed, the new movement gathered momentum. In the space of three days in July, the Clash and the Damned made their debut appearances supporting the Pistols. In September, the now-legendary Punk Rock Festival took place at the 100 Club, with the Pistols headlining and an early version of Siouxsie and the Banshees (with future Pistol

Below: The Sex Pistols.

Sid Vicious on drums) making their first appearance. By the end of the year, the Pistols, meanwhile, had signed to major label EMI, and released their first single 'Anarchy In The UK'.

At the beginning of December, the Pistols and friends appeared on the *Today* show, and outraged Middle England with a foul-mouthed outburst that dominated the following day's headlines, and cost host Bill Grundy his job. The TV station was inundated with complaints, and one angry viewer put his foot through his television screen in disgust!

April

The beginning of the month saw a British victory in the *Eurovision Song Contest*, as Brotherhood of Man swept the competition aside with 'Save Your Kisses For Me'. Only the French entry, Catherine Ferry's 'Un, Deux, Trois' came close, just 17 points behind, while third-placed Monaco trailed by a massive 69 points.

Taking the maximum score from seven national juries – Switzerland, Israel, Belgium, Norway, Greece, Spain and Portugal – 'Save Your Kisses For Me' had only narrowly been selected as the UK entry, with only a few more votes than the runner-up by Coco, who would themselves represent the UK in 1978.

Above: The Brotherhood Of Man.

The group's Lee Sheriden later summed up the song's impact – 'We'd had hits before *Eurovision*, but winning the contest just put a cap on all of it. "Save Your Kisses For Me" sold over 5 million records and was Number 1 in 31 countries, which was just wonderful, and we've been able to build from that ever since.'

May

The Who played their way into the *Guinness Book of Records* this month, after their performance at Charlton Athletic Football Club in South London was declared 'the loudest ever by a rock group' at 120 decibels. With Little Feat, the Sensational Alex Harvey Band, Streetwalkers, the Outlaws and Widowmaker in support,

the Who used a specially-built PA system that included seventy-two speakers and one hundred amplifiers delivering a total of 75,000 watts for the first of three football stadium gigs billed as 'The Who Put The Boot In'.

The 76,000 fans who braved the rain were also treated to a light show that cost an estimated £100,000, and introduced lasers to rock and roll for the first time. Sadly, though, the gigs weren't an unqualified success – in London, there were violent outbreaks and much confusion due to forged tickets and gatecrashing. Many fans with legitimate tickets were turned away, although they were compensated by a free coach ride to the show in Swansea two weeks later. And at the Celtic Park gig on 6 June, support band Streetwalkers were bottled off the stage.

SPORT

Montreal Olympics

As with many Olympic Games, the event staged in Montreal in July 1976 made headlines for political and as well as sporting reasons. The IOC refused to discipline New Zealand for their rugby tour of racially-segregated South Africa, resulting in a boycott by 32 African nations. The Montreal games saw women able to compete in basketball, rowing and team handball for the first time and hockey was played on an artificial pitch.

Below: Pete Townshend songwriter and guitarist with The Who, performing on stage.

As Olga Korbut had endeared herself to the world four years earlier, the star of these Games was Romanian Nadia Comaneci. The 14-year-old gymnast became the first to ever be awarded a perfect 10.00 score on her way to gold in the asymmetric bars. She also claimed gold in the all-around individual and balance beam events and bronze in the floor exercises to go with her silver in the combined exercises team, registering another six perfect scores along the way.

American boxers Ray Leonard and brothers Michael and Leon Spinks won gold in the light welterweight, middleweight and light heavyweight categories respectively before going on to enjoy successful professional careers.

Brendan Foster secured Britain's only track and field medal when he came third in the 10,000 metres but there was a success story in the swimming pool. David Wilkie won the 200 metres breaststroke gold to claim Britain's first men's swimming gold since Henry Taylor in 1908. Wilkie also came second in the 100 metres breaststroke.

Boxer Patrick Cowdell won the bantamweight bronze while David Starbrook (light heavyweight bronze) and

Above: Nadia Comaneci in action on the assymetrical bars.
Middle: Brendan Foster, (left), competing during the 1976 Montreal Olympics.
Below: Boxers Sugar Ray Leonard, (left), and Limazov Valbry during a match between the USA and USSR at the Montreal Olympics.

REMEMBER THE SEVENTIES

Keith Remfry (open silver) continued Britain's tradition of judo medals. The men's rowers picked up silver medals in the double sculls and eights while yachting enjoyed two medals: gold in the Tornado and silver in the Flying Dutchman classes.

James Hunt Formula 1 Champion

On 24 October 1976, the enigmatic James Hunt captured the Formula 1 world motor-racing title to fulfil his dream. His third place finish in the Japanese Grand Prix – after Championship leader Niki Lauda had retired because of the wet conditions – gave him the title by a single point.

James Simon Wallis Hunt was born on 29 August 1947 into a respectable London stockbroker family and enjoyed a public school education. Deciding at the age of 18 that a motor racing career was his ambition after seeing a meeting at Silverstone, Hunt progressed through Formula 3 – where he earned the nickname Hunt the Shunt – and Formula 2 culminating

Below: James Hunt leads the field in heavy rain at the Japanese Grand Prix, October 1976.

in a Formula 1 berth in the Hesketh team for the 1974 season.

He moved to McLaren in 1976 and scored a pole position in the first Grand Prix in Brazil, a race he would not finish due to car failure. He earned a second place in South Africa and took his first McLaren victory at Spain in the fourth race. He was initially stripped of his victory because his car was found to be too wide but this was reinstated on appeal.

Further victories followed in France, Britain – he was disqualified from the latter after restarting the race in a spare car following a shunt with Ferrari's Clay Regazzoni – and Germany. It was at the Nürburgring that Lauda crashed and suffered horrendous burns which would keep him out for six weeks.

Hunt used Lauda's absence to his advantage, claiming the chequered flag in Holland before his rival returned to the cockpit at Monza. Further victories in Canada and the United States set the scene for a thrilling finale.

Hunt retired in 1979 and enjoyed a successful career as a TV commentator before he died of a massive heart attack at the age of 45 on 15 June 1993.

John Curry wins two gold medals

Early 1976 was a spectacular time for ice skater John Curry. On 11 February he claimed Britain's first men's figure skating medal when he won gold at the Innsbruck Winter Olympic Games and he followed that achievement less than a month later by winning the World Figure Skating Championship in Stockholm.

Above: John Curry performs his program during the men's figure skating competition at the World Championships, March 1976.

Curry, born on 9 September 1949 in Birmingham, had aspired to be a ballet dancer as a child but his father did not approve so he tried his hand at skating and went on to become one of the best the world has seen. He was also awarded the OBE for his achievements.

Publicly 'outed' by a German magazine before the 1976 Games, Curry was open about his sexuality but was diagnosed with HIV in 1987. This developed into AIDS three years later and he died of a heart attack on 15 April 1994 at the age of 45.

POLITICS & CURRENT AFFAIRS

Wilson resigns

On 16 March 1976, Harold Wilson shocked the nation by resigning as prime minister. It seemed that no-one, not even his closest Cabinet colleagues, had been expecting the announcement. He said, however, that he had always intended to resign when he was 60, as by then he would be both physically and mentally exhausted. By 1976 he had been in parliament for a total of 31 years, had been leader of the Labour Party for 13 years, and prime minister for almost eight. He was his party's longest serving premier until this record was broken by Tony Blair in 2005.

When he resigned, Wilson assured the nation that there were 'no hidden reasons' for his departure, but he also said: 'I wish I could have been prime minister in happier times and easier times'. In fact, the times had been particularly difficult. Constant conflict with the unions, devaluation of the pound in 1967, rampant inflation during the early-1970s, and the somewhat ludicrous accusations that he was in fact a Soviet spy, had all taken their toll on Harold Wilson. He had however presided over the general liberalisation of a fast changing society, and had earned himself many admirers.

Above: John Curry waves to the crowd after winning the gold medal at the 1976 Winter Olympics.

1970 1971 1972 1973 1974 1975 1976

At the age of sixty, Wilson was actually still quite young by the standards of the twentieth century, but he did have a secret. He had begun to realise that he was suffering from the onset of Alzheimer's disease. His memory and powers of concentration, which had both been unsurpassed, were now beginning to fail him. This troubled him greatly, and he realised it was time to go. A few weeks after Wilson's resignation, James Callaghan became prime minister.

Harold Wilson was given a life peerage in 1983. He seldom appeared in public during his last years, and he died in 1995. His widow, Mary, lives on.

A year of deaths

An awful lot of well-known people died in 1976. In January, Chou En-Lai, China's prime minister since the communist revolution of 1949, died at the age of 78. Chou had been second in command to Chairman Mao, but for some reason his passing seemed to generate little interest in China itself. It was however a very different story a few months later, when Mao himself died. Mao Tse-Tung, the 'founder and wise leader of the Communist Party of China, the Chinese People's Liberation Army, and the People's Republic of China' died at the age of 82 in September. There were eight

Above: Harold Wilson on his way to Buckingham Palace to hand his resignation to the Queen.

days of official mourning and, on the day of his funeral, 800 million Chinese observed three minutes silence in memory of the man who had probably exerted influence on more people than anyone else in the twentieth century. A month or so later Mao's widow, along with

recluse in his later years, had in his younger days designed planes and set speed records. He had made movies and had also made a fortune from Las Vegas casinos. At his death, he was reported to be worth $1.5 million. In June,

the other members of the so-called 'Gang of Four' was jailed for supposedly plotting a coup. An official Chinese news agency report described the gang members as 'filthy and contemptible like dog's dung'.

While Chinese communist leaders were leaving this world, two of its richest men were also preparing to depart. In April, Howard Hughes, a strangely enigmatic American billionaire, died of a stroke on board his aeroplane at the age of seventy. Hughes, a remarkable

another eccentric American billionaire died: J Paul Getty, who had married and divorced five times, died at his home near London. He had made his money from oil – and he had held on to most of it.

Above left: Mao Tse Tung, Chinese Communist leader and the principal founder of the People's Republic of China.
Above right: American oil executive and art collector, John Paul Getty.

Riots stop the carnival

'This was supposed to be about fun and love' – so said one of the organisers, after the Notting Hill Carnival riots 30 years ago. Notting Hill, in London, had staged an annual carnival since 1964, but in August 1976 trouble erupted when the police attempted to arrest a pickpocket in Portobello Road, on the second day of the celebrations. A group of men attacked the police, and things soon got out of hand.

There had been a history of racial tension in the area, and the carnival was designed to involve all Londoners and celebrate the culture of the Caribbean community. In 1976 about a hundred police were injured, as well as 60 carnival goers. For a time it seemed that future celebrations of this kind were doomed, but happily the carnival later became the established, and largely peaceful, celebration that we know today.

Above: The aftermath of the Notting Hill Carnival, the Notting Hill riots.

1970 1971 1972 1973 1974 1975 1976 1977 1978 1979

1977

FASHION, CULTURE & ENTERTAINMENT

Disco, *Saturday Night Fever* and John Travolta

Influenced by soul, funk and Motown, disco music catered for nightclub and dancing audiences rather than general radio listeners. But its popularity peaked between 1977 and 1979.

The most popular disco artists of the time were the Bee Gees, Abba, Sister Sledge, the Jacksons, Donna Summer, Grace Jones, Boney M, Village People, KC and the Sunshine

Band, Barry White and Kool & the Gang. Typical disco music had an easy to follow rhythmic bass with a distinctive four/four beat. It was also the first time in more than three decades that orchestral music became popular again in popular music.

Above: Abba. From left to right: Benny Andersson, Anni-Frid Lyngstad, Agnetha Faltskog and Bjorn Ulvaeus.
Below: Disco poses.

114

Star Wars

Star Wars brought one of the most popular, profitable, entertaining and successful sci-fi movies of all time to the big screen. Directed by George Lucas, the film was shot on location in Tunisia, California's Death Valley and Guatemala. It showed advanced special-effects that had never been seen before and featured stunning music from composer John Williams.

Influenced by earlier films in the genre, including *Buck Rogers* and *Flash Gordon*, George Lucas had originally wanted to remake *Flash Gordon*, but the rights had been bought and he used the comic book character for inspiration instead along with *Forbidden Planet* (1940) and *2001: A Space Odyssey* (1968). He was also influenced by James Bond and the medieval knights of the round table and the story of Camelot. Lucas also followed the Greek tradition

Producers were all-important in the disco movement, the likes of Germany's Frank Farian (Boney M) and Giorgio Moroder (Donna Summer) and the Chic Organisation in the States (Diana Ross, Sister Sledge) shaping the sound if not themselves singing the songs. Beats per minute were all-important to keep the dance floor moving, with extended 12-inch singles the order of the day.

Below: C3PO and R2D2.

1970 1971 1972 1973 1974 1975 1976 1977 1978 1979

_1972 1973 1974 1975 1976 1977 1978 1979_

of beginning his epic in the middle – the first film in his original trilogy is in fact the fourth film in the entire series.

The film is a mythological tale of heroism and good overcoming evil starring Carrie Fisher (Princess Leia), Sir Alec Guinness (Obi Wan Kenobi) and the voice of James Earl Jones as Darth Vader, while David Prowse wears the suit. Comic performances come in the guise of robotic droids – R2D2 and C3P0. Harrison Ford also stars, as a mercenary space-pilot, while Mark Hamill plays Luke Skywalker (son of Anakin Skywalker who turned to the Dark Side and became Darth Vader) who is fighting the dark forces of the Empire.

The first film grossed $1.5 million in its opening weekend and $780 million overall. It was nominated for 10 Academy Awards and won six in technical categories.

Trimphone

In 1977, BT's luxury trimphone was given a face-lift – its dial was removed and it was given buttons instead. Due to the GPO monopoly of the time it was only possible to rent the trimphone, but you could opt for various coloured phones to brighten up your bedside table. Trimphone stood for Tone Ringer Illuminated Model and all were fitted with a tone ringer which started quietly but gradually got louder.

The GPO took a while to perfect the trimphone which was created in 1964, although trials of the phone didn't take place until the following year. The first actual trimphone was the ten millionth telephone to be rented and it was presented to newlyweds in 1965 by the Postmaster General. After a dubious start and unsuccessful trials the trimphone was available nationwide by 1968.

The Krypton Factor

Hosted by Gordon Burns, ITV's _Krypton Factor_ was TV's quest to find the cleverest, fittest and most dextrous person in the UK. Faced with giant jigsaws, assault courses and various other brainteasers, contestants took part in a show that was one of the few on ITV to run without commercials in its 30-minute slot.

Each show consisted of six rounds, including observation skills, mental agility, physical fitness –

Below: Tony Benn tries out a luxury 'Trimphone'.

tackling an army training course – and a simulation exercise where contestants were expected to fly and land a huge aircraft. There was also a logic round where an obscure shape needed to be built, but there were no directions on how to make the shape, and a general knowledge quick-fire quiz. Three of the rounds were designed so that those watching could also participate. *The Krypton Factor* remained popular for 18 years.

Skateboards

It is generally believed that skateboards were created in the 1950s by Californian surfers who attached roller skates to long boards. Side-walk surfing, as it was known, was considered inferior to surfing the waves, but by 1977 skateboarding was a skill that many in the UK were keen to have. Requiring balance, good footwork and attitude, perhaps the greatest impact of skateboarding is the 'slacker' fashion that accompanied the sport.

The first commercial skateboard went on sale in 1959 called the Roller Derby Skateboard (no doubt named after the roller skating craze of 1950s' America). Six years later, an estimated 50 million skateboards had

been sold. By today's standards the boards were primitive and around an inch thick with hard clay or rubber wheels. A cult soon developed and more 'designer' boards were introduced including the Hobie – established in 1964 by Hobie Alter, the surfing legend.

Written and directed by Noel Black, the first skateboarding movie *Skaterdater* was released in 1965 and styles began to be developed including freestyle, slalom, downhill and high and long jumping. Skateboarding became known as the urban rebel's pastime and even the high-tech dedicated skating parks around today have done little to dispel the myth.

MUSIC

January

No-one took too much notice of the New York Magazine's cover story on 7 June 1976. Titled *'Tribal Rites Of The New Saturday Night'*, Nik Cohn's story

Above: A skateboarder rides his skateboard.
Below: John Travolta sits beside a promotional poster of himself from the film 'Saturday Night Fever'.

about the mid-1970s disco scene, and one particular character called Vincent, was probably forgotten within a few days by the vast majority of those who read it.

By chance, though, the story was spotted by producer Robert Stigwood, who decided it would provide a good basis for a film about the NY disco scene, and an ideal vehicle for young actor John Travolta, then under contract to Stigwood. By January 1977, plans were well advanced, but the question of music had to

be settled. With this in mind, Stigwood approached another of his roster of artists, the Bee Gees, and asked them to write some material for the film.

The rest is history. *Saturday Night Fever* opened in December, and the accompanying soundtrack double album spent most of the following year topping the charts on both sides of the Atlantic – unsurprisingly, it would soon become the biggest-selling soundtrack album of all time, and remains so today. 'Vincent', of

Above: John Travolta as Tony Manero, disco dancing in the film 'Saturday Night Fever'.

course, became the film's main character, Tony Manero... John Travolta became a megastar almost overnight, the Bee Gees never looked back, and *Saturday Night Fever* went on to gross almost $250,000,000 worldwide.

In an amazing twist, Nik Cohn admitted in 1997 that much of the original magazine article was pure fiction. On the occasion of the film's twentieth anniversary, British-born Cohn described how he'd been assigned to write an article about the NY disco boom, and had gone to Brooklyn's famous 2001 Odyssey club to do some research. 'I didn't learn much...I made a lousy interviewer: I knew nothing about this world, and it showed. Quite literally, I didn't speak the language,' he confessed. 'So I faked it. I conjured up the story of the figure in the doorway, and named him Vincent...I wrote it all up. And presented it as fact...'

Keith Richards rolled into court this month to be fined £750 for a drugs offence committed last May when police had found cocaine and LSD in his Bentley. The Rolling Stones guitarist *had* driven it into the central reservation of the M1 near Newport Pagnell, Bucks...at 5 a.m. in the morning! His claim that the group shared clothes

and so the offending substances could have been anyone's was challenged by the police, who showed a photo of him on stage wearing a tube-like necklace that had contained the coke.

He was eventually cleared of the LSD charge but convicted of cocaine possession – a verdict he described, while celebrating with Mick Jagger in the pub afterwards, as 'a good old-fashioned British compromise.' Unfortunately for the human riff, his untidy habits would catch up with him again the very next month when Mounties seized quantities of substances suspected to be heroin and cocaine while he was in Toronto to complete recording of the 'Love You Live' album.

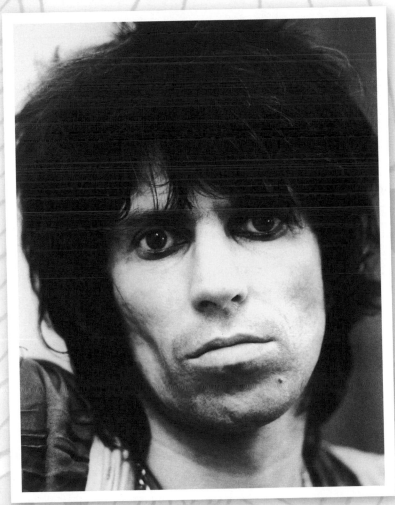

Below: Portrait of Keith Richards.

One month after they scandalised middle-class Britain by swearing on screen, the Sex Pistols were given their marching orders by record company EMI – together with a tasty £50,000 pay-off. Not that it bothered Johnny Rotten and company overmuch: though widely banned in Britain, their February tour of Europe remained firmly on, while a number of rival companies were known to be anxious to secure their services.

The latest outrage that provoked the order of the boot was their behaviour at London's Heathrow Airport en-route to a show in Amsterdam. 'What are ashtrays for but to spit in?' asked Rotten – aka John Lydon – in his 1993 autobiography. 'You do that, some old woman gets offended and there's forty journalists to blow it out of all proportion. Okay, Steve (Jones) did vomit in Heathrow…but why was it news?' EMI, who'd be commemorated by a track of that name on the Pistols' first album, were undoubtedly the losers in the affair.

And the label's withdrawn version of 'Anarchy In The UK' would become an instant collector's item.

August

On 16 August, the world said farewell to The King. Elvis Presley, whose singing style revolutionised popular music in the 1950s, was dead at 42.

Presley was rushed to Baptist Memorial Hospital in Memphis, Tennessee after being found slumped on the floor of a bathroom in Graceland by his girlfriend, 20-year-old Ginger Alden. He was pronounced dead on arrival, and one of rock'n'roll's all time greats was gone. Within hours of the announcement of his death, tributes poured in, radio stations flooded the

Above: The Sex Pistols with their manager Malcolm McLaren (third from right) signing a new contract with A&M Records outside Buckingham Palace after being dropped from EMI.

airwaves with his records, and prominent public figures from around the world made suitably reverential statements. US President Jimmy Carter said, 'Elvis Presley's death deprives our country of a part of itself. He was unique and irreplaceable. His music and his personality, fusing the styles of white country and black rhythm and blues, permanently changed the face of American popular culture.' Former President Richard Nixon asked all Americans to fly their flags at half-mast, while distraught fans bought $400 million-worth of Presley's records. In the UK, 'Way Down' became his first Number 1 single since 1970.

Outside Graceland there were chaotic scenes, with 300 women and children requiring medical attention, and 80,000 making a pilgrimage to the singer's home. A public viewing of the body was arranged for the next day. Dressed in a cream suit, white tie, and pale blue shirt, Elvis lay in state in a heavy copper coffin – it was the first time Graceland had been open to the public since Presley had bought it in 1957. Having seen their idol, many fans collapsed.

Almost immediately, the conspiracy theories began, many based on the

Above: Elvis Presley poses for a portrait.
Below: Graceland, the Elvis Presley mansion in Memphis, Tennessee.

idea that the death had been faked, and the King was still alive and well… almost thirty years on, Elvis sightings are still reported from time to time, although how many can be ascribed to the thriving Elvis impersonation industry can only be guessed.

The cause of death was initially given as a heart attack, and Tennessee state pathologist, Dr Jerry Francisco, claimed that there was 'no sign of any drug abuse'. Later reports confirmed that the primary cause of death was actually polypharmacy, with one indicating the detection of fourteen drugs in Elvis's system, 'ten in significant quantity', although ill-health may have increased the singer's dependency on prescription medication.

September

Exactly a month after Elvis', another sudden death shook the music world when it was announced that Marc Bolan had died in a car accident just two weeks short of his thirtieth birthday. His car, driven by his girlfriend Gloria Jones, struck a tree in Barnes, south-west London, close to his home in Richmond.

Above: Two female fans attend the funeral of Marc Bolan at Golders Green Crematorium, London.
Below: The wrecked Mini 1275 GT in which Marc Bolan died when it collided with a tree on Barnes Common.

1977 had seen something of a revival in Bolan's fortunes – his latest album, 'Dandy In The Underworld', had attracted favourable reviews and charted briefly in the UK, and the accompanying tour, featuring punk-rockers The Damned as support, had also been well-received. In the weeks before his death, he'd hosted his own ITV show, *Marc*, allowing him to showcase new talent while bringing his own music to a fresh, younger audience.

On the final show, which proved to be his last public appearance, he sang a duet with his old friend David Bowie.

Bolan had lost weight, looked sharper than for many moons, and seemed set to revitalise a career that had lain dormant for several years, but any hopes of future success were tragically wiped out early on the morning of 16 September.

SPORT

Australia and England play Centenary Test

The cricket teams of Australia and England met in a Test match held in Melbourne in March 1977 to commemorate the 100th anniversary of the first Test meeting of the two countries. In 1877, Australia had won by 45 runs.

Australia batted first in the Centenary Test and were dismissed for 138 runs but Dennis Lillee wreaked havoc on the English batsmen, finishing the first innings with six wickets and giving away a measly 26 runs. The hosts put on a much better showing in their second innings, eventually declaring on 419-9 with Rodney Marsh (110 not out) becoming the first Australian wicket-keeper to register a century against England. Despite Derek Randall scoring his first Test century (174), the visitors could only amass 417 runs and so lost the match by a coincidental 45 runs.

A second Centenary Test was contested at Lord's in 1980 to commemorate the first meeting of the two sides on English soil but rain disrupted play and the match was drawn.

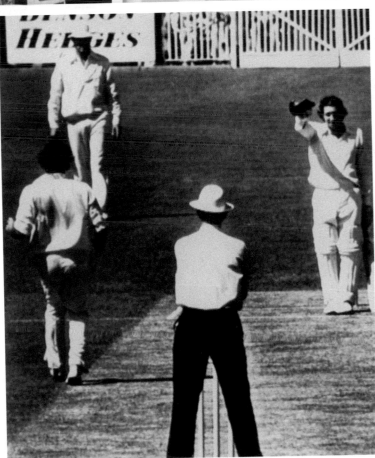

Below: Action during the centenary test match against Australia in Melbourne, March 1977.

1970 1971 1972 1973 1974 1975 1976 1977 1978 1979

Pelé plays final game

The world said a fond farewell to the greatest footballer ever seen on 1 October 1977 when Pelé played his last game as a professional. He had signed for New York Cosmos three years earlier and had proved an unbelievable crowd-puller alongside fellow Brazilian Carlos Alberto and Germany's Franz Beckenbauer.

His last match was played against his former club Santos and he played the first half and scored for the Americans then switched to the Brazilians for the rest of the game. He did turn out in a few more friendly games for the New York club after this match but declined an offer from Cosmos to come out of retirement.

Edson Arantes do Nascimento was born on 23 October 1940 and first came to global attention as the then youngest player to ever appear and score in a World Cup when he helped Brazil to lift the Jules Rimet trophy in Sweden in 1958.

He went on to play in three more World Cup tournaments. Brazil successfully defended their crown in Chile four years later but Pelé did not play in the Final after aggravating a groin injury in the opening stages of the competition. He suffered with injury again in 1966 as Brazil failed to negotiate the group phase but returned at his best in Mexico four years later. He scored once in the Final against Italy and set up another for Carlos Alberto as Brazil on 4-1 and became the first nation to win three World Cups.

Pelé was unable to take his talents to Europe at club level because the Brazilian government declared him a national treasure early in his career to prevent

Below: Pelé being presented with an engraved silver salver to mark his retirement after his last match in New York, 1st October 1977.

him being transferred out of the country. He finished his career with an amazing 1,281 goals in 1,363 games and has since become an ambassador for the sport.

Bjorn Borg retains Wimbledon title

Swedish sensation Bjorn Borg dominated world tennis for the latter half of the 1970s and appeared in six consecutive Wimbledon Finals between 1976-81 in his brief professional career.

On 2 July 1977, he met American Jimmy Connors in the Centre Court showpiece and retained the title he had won the previous year in a five-set thriller (3-6, 0-2, 0-1, 5-7, 8-4). Indeed, this match and his semi-final clash with Vitas Gerulaitis (6-4, 3-6, 6-3, 3-6, 8-6) have been pronounced by many as the best ever seen at Wimbledon.

The young Bjorn Rune Borg, born on 6 June 1956 in Sodertaljie, was fascinated by a tennis racquet his

Above: Bjorn Borg holds up the men's singles trophy for the second year running after beating Jimmy Connors in the final at Wimbledon.

father had won in a table tennis tournament and the love affair began. He became the youngest winner of the Italian and French Championships in 1974 and reached the quarter-final stage in his first Wimbledon tournament the following year. Losing to eventual winner Arthur Ashe, Borg then remained unbeaten for 41 consecutive matches.

He had become the youngest Wimbledon winner for 45 years with his victory over Ilie Nastase in the 1976 tournament and would hold the title for five years with Final wins over Connors again (in 1978), Roscoe Tanner (1979) and John McEnroe (1980).

It would be McEnroe who would end Borg's winning streak and prevent him from equalling the record six consecutive titles won by Willie Renshaw in the 1880s. The American also defeated Borg in the US Open Final, claiming his Number 1 spot and the Swede retired in 1982 at the age of 26.

He finished his career with a record six French Open titles but failed to win the US Open despite appearing in four Finals. He only entered the fourth Grand Slam tournament – the Australian Open – once, reaching the third round in 1974. Borg was inducted into the Tennis Hall of Fame in 1987 and attempted a series of comebacks in the early 1990s without success.

POLITICS & CURRENT AFFAIRS

Queen's Silver Jubilee

The Queen celebrated her silver jubilee on 6 February 1977, 25 years after the death of her father King George VI. As it is hardly customary to organise a public celebration of someone's death, the actual festivities took place a few months later. Accordingly, on 7 June, everybody turned out to thank Her Majesty for a quarter of a century of service to her people.

The royal family had endured its share of troubles over the years, and the Queen's immediate family had many more to come. But still, most people, except perhaps the more die-hard republicans, felt that she had done a pretty good job, and a goodly turnout was expected for the royal progress in the golden state coach to St Paul's Cathedral. Unfortunately, it rained a lot, but this didn't stop more than a million people lining

the streets along the way. Many had been there all night, and some probably caught pneumonia, but it was all in a good cause. The purveyors of plastic rainwear made a fortune.

The procession wended its way down the Mall, across Trafalgar Square, down Fleet Street and up Ludgate Hill. The Queen wore pink. There were 2,700 specially invited guests at St Paul's, including a variety of prime ministers and other Commonwealth leaders. There was a lunch at the Guildhall, and later there was a good deal of mingling with the crowds. Having received enough flowers to fill both Buckingham Palace and Windsor Castle, the Queen thanked the people of Britain and the Commonwealth for their loyalty and friendship during the 25 years.

Above: Residents of a Fulham estate express their sentiments in a celebration of the Queen's Silver Jubilee.

1970 1971 1972 1973 1974 1975 1976 1977 1978 1979

The nation celebrated with street parties, while the Sex Pistols (who had not been invited to St Paul's) sailed down the Thames, playing their particular version of 'God Save The Queen.' They were arrested as they left the boat.

Steve Biko killed

Stephen Bantu Biko is regarded as having been the founder of the Black consciousness movement in South Africa, and one of its many martyrs. Born in 1946, Biko was a rebel from the start, having been expelled from his first school for 'anti-establishment behaviour'. He later went to the University of Natal Medical School (Black Section) where, as far as he was able to, he became involved with student politics – before being expelled once more.

In 1972 Steve Biko became a founder member of the Black People's Convention. Throughout the rest of his short life he devoted himself to anti-apartheid activities. Between 1975 and 1977 he was arrested and interrogated on four occasions under South African anti-terrorism legislation, and in August 1977 he was detained by the Eastern Cape security police in Port Elizabeth. In September, he was subjected to interrogation at the security police headquarters, where he mysteriously sustained a head injury. Unsurprisingly, he then became even more unco-operative than usual, and started to act strangely. He was

Above: The body of South African political leader Steve Biko.
Below: Several anti-apartheid militants attending the burial ceremony of Steve Biko.

examined by doctors, but they failed to note any signs of neurological injury.

A few days later Biko was found in a semi-conscious state, and the police physician recommended that he be transferred to a hospital immediately. Instead, he was driven 1,200 km to Pretoria Central Prison, apparently naked and in the back of a Land Rover. Steve Biko died from brain injuries a few hours later. At first, it was suggested that he had died following a hunger strike, with all the medical evidence – and the likelihood that he had been deliberately beaten up – being completely ignored. When the truth emerged, the South African government suffered further world-wide condemnation. There can be little doubt that the killing of Steve Biko helped to hasten the end of the Apartheid regime.

Spanish democracy

Spain had been led by the right-wing dictator General Franco since before World War Two but, on 15 June 1977, the country held its first free elections since 1936. Franco had died in 1975 and now the Spanish people were to be able to elect the government of their choice. The Spanish Civil War had been between Franco's Fascists and the Communists, but by 1977 extremism was out of favour. The election was won by the Democratic Centre coalition, led by Adolfo Suarez, which polled 6.31 million votes (34.5% - 166 seats). Next came the Socialists with 5.37 million votes (29.4% - 118 seats) with the Communist Party and the right- wing Popular Alliance each netting less than 2 million votes.

Spain was a democracy once more, and everyone could go there for their holidays without worrying about the political situation. Not that many holidaymakers had worried about it in the first place.

1970 1971 1972 1973 1974 1975 1976 1977 1978 1979

Below: Adolfo Suarez, the winner of the Spanish election.

1978

FASHION, CULTURE & ENTERTAINMENT

New Wave

In 1978, the new punk look was created when the New Wave culture crept onto the scene. The music and fashion of New Wave had all the aggressiveness and menace of its predecessor but reverted to the old Teddy Boy style of the 1950s. Leather and ripped jeans – and all over body piercing – gave way to sharp suits, brothel creepers, mohair and slim jim ties. Emulated by bands like the Jam and the Boomtown Rats the vibrant music era lasted from 1978–82.

Formed in 1978, Dexy's Midnight Runners were another New Wave pop and soul band who – although lacking the sharp suits – still took the new era by storm. After punk rock, New Wave was less noisy and more pop-orientated and much of the music was manufactured, while post-punk was darker and featured less pop-inspired groups.

Music of the 1970s was by now considered overproduced and uninspired. Punk, post-punk and New Wave were all designed as a reaction to this and most bands of the time could easily fit into more than one of these genres. Primarily showing in nightclubs, videos of New Wave bands helped to promote the music and most bands took advantage of it. The real boost came when MTV began broadcasting in 1981 and nearly all music videos were of New Wave bands. Although New Wave was thought to have had its day in the mid-1980s, the music continued to influence later bands and artists up until the early 1990s.

Above: Bob Geldof, lead singer of The Boomtown Rats on stage at the Hammersmith Odeon, London.

Dallas

Dallas was one of the biggest prime-time dramas that caught the attention of soap-opera audiences all over the world. Set in *Dallas*, Texas, it told the story of the wealthy Ewing family and their oil business. It first aired in a five week run on Sunday nights in early 1978, but was moved to a slot on Saturday nights later in the year.

Although popular, *Dallas* didn't become a must-see until it was given a Friday-night slot one year later and ratings were high. It was aired on CBS network in the US and ran for 14 seasons from 2 April 1978 to 3 May 1991. By the early 1980s, *Dallas* had become one of the most popular TV shows in history.

Creator David Jacobs wrote the show when his earlier series Knots Landing was considered not glamourous enough by CBS. After the success of *Dallas*, CBS decided to make Knots Landing a spin-off. South Fork, a sprawling ranch in Braddock County, was the the family home. Patriarch Jock Ewing and his wife Miss Ellie raised three sons at South Fork and it was Jacobs's intention that the series should centre around the youngest, Bobby (Patrick Duffy), and his relationship with his wife Pamela Barnes, (Victoria Principal), daughter of the Ewing's biggest business rival.

However, the popularity of oldest son, JR, played by Larry Hagman, really took off and the scheming, underhand oil baron became the focus of the show along with wife Sue Ellen, played by Linda Gray. Life of middle son Gary was the focus of the spin-off *Knots Landing*.

With plenty of intrigue, romance and sex, cowboy antics and business rivalry *Dallas* had a formula that delighted its audience

Below: Larry Hagman as JR Ewing in a promotional portrait for the television series, Dallas.

and made it successful for its entire run. Each season always ended with the most outrageous cliff-hanger which left fans in suspense until the start of the following season.

Anna Ford, the first female newsreader to join ITN

On 13 February 1978, Anna Ford, former reporter and presenter of *Tomorrow's World*, joined Independent Television News (ITN) as their first female newsreader. She was ITV's answer to the BBC's Angela Rippon who presented the *Nine O'Clock News*. But when ITN announced that Ford was joining the team, the BBC immediately took legal action against her for breach of contract. Following a legal battle which took place behind the scenes, the BBC agreed to release the then 34-year-old from her 12-month contract (which still had ten months to run). ITN were reportedly paying Ford a starting salary of £14,000 compared with the £10,000 she was earning with the BBC.

Anna Ford made her debut on the news on the *News At Ten* programme on 9 March. Having gained a BA honours degree in economics at Manchester University, Ford went on to become a tutor in social studies at the Open University in Northern Ireland. She later joined Granada Television as a researcher before joining the BBC's documentary series, *Man Alive*. Her stint as a newsreader ended in 2006 when she left to explore other career opportunities.

Lycra and jogging – the perfect match

1978 saw the start of the UK's first jogging craze where outfits were made of Lycra, and lots of it. Lycra was made of stretch fibre which, combined with other fabrics, gave the wearer a close fit, comfort and freedom of movement – ideal for all those fitness fanatics running in parks and up and down pavements across the UK. With a remarkable ability to stretch up to 600% per cent and back again to its original shape, Lycra provided versatility. It can be combined with virtually every other fibre, including natural and manmade, giving different levels of stretch and versatility.

Whether you actually exercised or not, it was cool to put on your jogging suit, Adidas (three-stripes) trainers and sweatband and go out in public. Despite the

Above: Anna Ford, the first woman newscaster on ITN.

Hence the 12-inch single, played at 45rpm to give a better treble sound, was born.

Gimmicks became the norm in the fight to secure sales and soon 12-inch singles hit the shops along with picture disc singles and one-sided singles. However, despite its revival and success in the late 1970s and early 1980s, the 12-inch single was never going to challenge new technology in the form of compact discs. Many albums now include a '12-inch version' as a bonus track.

New Order have the honour of releasing the biggest selling 12-inch single of all time with 1983's 'Blue Monday', helped by the fact that their record label Factory didn't release it as a 7-inch.

MUSIC

April

The combination of popular music and politics has a long and chequered history, stretching from the protest songs of Woody Guthrie to modern rap artists and the use of familiar songs in today's mainstream political campaigns.

This month, though, saw the start of one of the most successful marriages of music and politics, when the Tom Robinson Band led an Anti-Nazi League march from Trafalgar Square to Hackney's Victoria Park, where an estimated 80,000 people watched the TRB, reggae band Steel Pulse, X-Ray Spex and the Clash play.

Rock Against Racism became one of the most important musical movements ever, focusing attention on the activities of the National Front, whose overtly

dramatic rise in inflation during the year, sales of jogging suits and other sportswear rocketed as the nation all joined in the fitness craze.

12-inch singles

It was the rise of disco in the late 1970s that brought about a change in the record industry. While the 7-inch single had long been the most popular format, songs were now longer and DJs wanted a better sound quality.

1970 1971 1972 1973 1974 1975 1976 1977 1978 1979

1970 1971 1972 1973 1974 1975 1976 1977 1978 1979

racist agenda was effectively marginalised as a result. Almost thirty years on, despite localised political success, the NF has never regained the ground it lost in the summer of 1978. During the year, two more RAR Carnivals took place, with Graham Parker & the Rumour, the Fall, Steel Pulse and Buzzcocks playing in Manchester's Alexandra Park in July, and Elvis Costello, Misty In Roots, Sham 69 and Aswad playing at the capital's second RAR event in Brixton's Brockwell Park in September.

The main catalyst for these events had come the previous autumn, when thousands of anti-fascists,

including large numbers of local black youths, prevented the National Front from marching through Lewisham, South London. The Anti-Nazi League had been set up soon after, and had quickly joined forces with another nascent anti-fascist movement, Rock Against Racism.

RAR had been formed after Eric Clapton's public expression of support for Tory MP Enoch Powell, considered by many as openly racist. Clapton's stance was seen as hypocritical – he had, after all, built a hugely successful career around the work of black musicians – and RAR was initially set up to counter the growth of racism in music.

Above: Thousands of teachers from Southall attend the funeral of Blair Peach, the New Zealander who died in the anti-National Front riots in Southall.
Below: Elvis Costello at the microphone.

Over the next few years, the ANL and RAR worked hard to change attitudes. There were setbacks – in April 1979, violence between ANL supporters and the Metropolitan Police's Special Patrol Group led to the death of teacher Blair Peach – but by the early-1980s the NF were in retreat and racist ideas were becoming less acceptable, and RAR was formally wound down late in 1981.

June

By mid-1978, punk rock was all but burned out, and music was moving on. Manchester would prove to be a fertile breeding ground for the next generation of bands, and the city's Factory label would soon come to be regarded as one of the most important independent outlets for the new music.

Before the label came into being, though, the Factory name had been associated with a Manchester club, the brainchild of TV presenter Tony Wilson and band manager Alan Erasmus. The Hacienda opened its doors this month, showcasing new local bands such as Joy Division and the Durutti Column, and featuring other performers like comedian John Dowie and Sheffield experimentalists Cabaret Voltaire.

Graphic artist Peter Saville produced posters advertising the club, and when Wilson and Erasmus decided to form Factory Records to release material by the acts appearing at the club, Saville became the label's designer. Over the years, Saville's work for Factory ensured his place as one of rock's most influential figures – not bad for someone who has never made or produced a record in his life…

July

Bob Dylan closed the European leg of his 1978 world tour with an extra show at Blackbushe Aerodrome, near

Below: Bob Dylan on stage during the Blackbushe Pop Festival, July 1978.

Camberley in Surrey, this month. Around 250,000 fans watched Lake, Joan Armatrading, Graham Parker & the Rumour and Eric Clapton before the legendary singer took the stage for almost three hours, closing with a version of 'Forever Young', for which Clapton joined him on stage.

Billed as 'The Picnic at Blackbushe', the gig was arranged for thousands of disappointed fans who'd been unable to get tickets for Dylan's Earl's Court gigs the previous month – the six consecutive nights at the London venue had been his first UK gigs in nine years, so demand had been phenomenal. On the opening night at Earl's Court, Dylan was on good form – the

press coverage was full of hyperbole, with the *Daily Mail*'s reviewer declaring it 'the greatest concert I have ever seen', and *The Sun*'s asserting that 'Dylan lives up to his legend'. Bootlegs of the Blackbushe concert confirm that he was still on top of his game musically, but the sound quality at the gig was poor, and many complained that it was difficult to hear their hero.

1978 was a high-profile year for Dylan, who had disappeared from view once his Rolling Thunder Revue had

Below: Music fans queue for tickets for the concert by Bob Dylan.

1970 1971 1972 1973 1974 1975 1976 1977 1978 1979

ground to a halt in the autumn of 1976. In the intervening period, Dylan had completed work on his film of the Rolling Thunder tour, Renaldo & Clara, become divorced from Sara, his wife of ten years, and written material for his latest album 'Street Legal', as well as preparing for his 1978 World Tour.

Renaldo & Clara opened to generally poor reviews in January, and it's not hard to see why – clocking in at four hours, it was an obscure mix of self-examination, pretentious play-acting and excellent footage from the

tour, but it was for fanatical Dylan followers only. 'Street Legal' fared rather better, especially in the UK, where his concert appearances boosted sales and the album only narrowly failed to top the chart.

September

Who drummer Keith Moon became rock's latest casualty early this month, when he died from an overdose of Chlormethiazole, ironically a drug he'd been prescribed to help him to combat his over-indulgence in

Above: Keith Moon with his girlfriend Annette Walter-Lax at the film premiere of The Buddy Holly Story in London, on what would be his last night out.

1979 1978 1977 1976 1975 1974 1973 1972 1971 1970

October

Sex Pistols bassist Sid Vicious was in serious trouble this month, arrested on a charge of second-degree murder after calling police to the room in New York's Chelsea Hotel he'd been sharing with girlfriend Nancy Spungen. Vicious allegedly woke from a drugged stupor on the morning of 12 October to find Spungen dead in a pool of blood on the bathroom

alcohol. There were rumours of suicide, but the subsequent inquest ruled that his death was due to 'accidental misadventure'. It's thought that Moon took his medication, which had tranquilizing qualities, fell asleep, then woke confused and took more, doing this several times before overdosing.

The previous evening, 32-year-old Moon and his girlfriend Annette Walter-Lax had been Paul McCartney's guests at a preview screening of the film *The Buddy Holly Story*, before returning to a flat they had on loan from singer-songwriter Harry Nilsson. Just four years earlier, Cass Elliot, singer with the Mamas and the Papas, had died in the same flat – this second tragedy was understandably too much for Nilsson, who sold the flat shortly afterwards.

'Moon the Loon', one of rock'n'roll's greatest characters, was gone – it's perhaps a shame that his hedonistic, hell-raising image still tends to overshadow his status as arguably the best rock drummer ever.

floor. She'd been stabbed once in the abdomen, and had bled to death.

Vicious initially insisted he had no memory of having stabbed Spungen, although he later claimed to have 'killed her because I'm a dirty dog.' There were also unsubstantiated theories that Spungen was murdered by someone else, usually said to be one of the two drug dealers who visited the hotel room that evening.

Above: A drum kit owned by Keith Moon from The Who.
Below: Sid Vicious on stage with his American girlfriend Nancy Spungen, 1978.

The truth will never be known. Vicious was bailed by manager Malcolm McLaren with $50,000 provided by Virgin Records. Within days, he had attempted to take his own life by slashing his wrists, and, in February 1979, he died of a heroin overdose, regarded by many as deliberate, before he could be brought to trial.

Dalglish and Archie Gemmell (2, including the goal of the tournament) gave the Tartan Army hope but the game finished 3-2 and the Scottish adventure was over for another four years.

Hosts Argentina – runners-up in the 1930 Final – registered 2-1 victories over Hungary and France before

SPORT

Argentina World Cup

Scotland were once again the sole Home Nations representatives in the 1978 football World Cup held in Argentina. Despite losing just one qualifier (2-0 in Italy), England had lost out to the Italians on goal difference while Wales and Northern Ireland had finished third in their respective groups.

A 3-1 defeat by Peru and a 1-1 draw with Iran meant that Scotland had to beat Holland by three goals to progress to the next phase. Goals from Kenny

going down 1-0 to Italy, but it was enough to progress to the next round while reigning Champions West Germany had mixed fortunes. They thrashed Mexico 6-0 but then drew 0-0 with Tunisia and Poland.

In the second phase, Holland beat Austria (5-1) and Italy (2-1) and drew with West Germany (2-2) to top their group while Argentina won against Poland (2-0) and Peru (6-0) and played out a stalemate with Brazil. Argentina went through to the Final on goal difference at Brazil's expense who finished third after beating Italy 2-1 with goals from Nelinho and Dirceu.

Above: The Argentinian team celebrate with the trophy after the World Cup final against Holland.

Scotland were the visitors to Cardiff Arms Park two weeks later and the first half was a close-fought affair with Wales edging in front 8-7 at the interval. The home side stepped up a gear in the second half, however, and finished the match 22-14 winners, their

Valencia's Mario Kempes, just 23 years old, had already scored four times in the tournament and predictably it was he who opened the scoring for Argentina after 38 minutes. Substitute Dick Nanninga levelled the match with eight minutes to go and Rob Rensenbrink could have secured the title for Holland but hit the post in injury time. Instead, it was Kempes who got his and Argentina's second in extra time and midfielder Daniel Bertoni ensured victory for the host nation 11 minutes later.

Wales win their second Grand Slam in three years

Welsh rugby was so dominant in the late 1970s that they won the Five Nations Championship on four occasions in five years between 1975–79. In two of those seasons, 1976 and 1978, they also completed the Grand Slam with victories against the other four nations.

The 1978 campaign kicked off with a visit to Twickenham, home of English rugby, on 4 February with scrum-half Gareth Edwards celebrating his 50th cap. It was a battle between the kickers with no tries being scored and Phil Bennett came out on top with three successful penalties to Alastair Hignell's two to give the Dragons a 9-6 victory.

four tries being scored by Edwards, Ray Gravell, Derek Quinnell and Steve Fenwick.

Wales visited Ireland's Lansdowne Road in the next fixture and battled hard to win 20-16. JJ Williams scored a try for the visitors and Fenwick took over the kicking duties from Bennett with four successful penalties to go with his own try.

So it was left to reigning Champions France to visit Cardiff on 18 March in an attempt to prevent a second Welsh Grand Slam in three years. It was Phil Bennett's last appearance in a Welsh jersey and he capped a magnificent career with two tries and a conversion.

Above: The scoreboard at the River Plate stadium announcing that Argentina have won the World Cup.
Below: Welsh Rugby Union player, Gareth Edwards, after receiving a golden boot at the Painter's Hall, London, for his performance in the Five Nations tournament.

Edwards and Fenwick were also on target with a drop goal each to give Wales a 16-7 victory and the Grand Slam.

Welsh rugby went into a period of decline during the 1980s and 1990s and they would have to wait another 27 years to claim a further Grand Slam title.

Liverpool retain European Cup

Liverpool became the sixth club to successfully defend their European Cup when they beat FC Bruges 1-0 at Wembley on 30 May 1978. The two clubs had last met in the 1976 UEFA Cup Final with the Merseysiders winning the two-legged tie 4-3 on aggregate.

Liverpool had secured their place in the Final with victories over Dresden, Benfica and Borussia Moenchengladbach and the only goal of a disappointing game was scored by Scottish midfielder Kenny Dalglish, signed the previous summer to replace Anfield legend Kevin Keegan.

It would prove to be the second year in a period of English domination that lasted six seasons in the competition. Liverpool had already beaten

Below: The players of Liverpool Football Club carry the trophy on a lap of honour after their 1-0 victory over FC Bruges in the European Cup final at Wembley Stadium.

1970 1971 1972 1973 1974 1975 1976 1977 1978 1979

Moenchengladbach 3-1 the previous year and triumphed again in 1980 (1-0 against Real Madrid) while Nottingham Forest (1979-80) and Aston Villa (1982) would ensure the coveted trophy temporarily remained out of reach of continental Europe.

POLITICS & CURRENT AFFAIRS

Moro murdered

In March 1978, the former Christian Democratic prime minister of Italy, Aldo Moro, was kidnapped in Rome as he was being driven to the parliament building. There had already been threats against his life, so he was accompanied by five police bodyguards, all of whom were shot and killed during the kidnapping. It seemed that up to a dozen gunmen took part in the attack, and they whisked Moro away.

The usual roadblocks and hovering helicopters made their appearance after the event, but to no avail. Before long, there was a 'phone call to a Rome newspaper from a member of the extreme left-wing 'Red Brigade', in which the caller demanded the suspension of an on-going trial of 15 members of that organisation. The trial was not suspended, and the Italian nation held its breath: Aldo Moro, aged 61, was a respected politician (no mean feat, in Italy) and trade unions called a 24-hour strike in protest at the kidnapping. This naturally had no effect on the Red Brigade, whose spokesman had already said:

'We kidnapped Aldo Moro. He is only our first victim. We shall hit at the heart of the state.'

Moro was kept at a secret location in Rome, from which he wrote letters to his family and to the government, asking the latter to negotiate his release. Various people, including Pope Paul VI, begged them to come to some kind of accommodation with the kidnappers, but the government stood firm. Two months after he was kidnapped, the bullet-ridden body of Aldo Moro was found in the boot of a car in central Rome. It took a long time to round them up, but by the mid-1980s most of the more prominent members of the Red Brigade had been arrested.

Below: Italian prime minister Aldo Moro after his abduction by the Red Brigade, who subsequently murdered him.

Year of three popes

Pope Paul VI, who had been the pontiff since 1963, died at the age of 80, following a heart attack on 6 August 1978. The Pope had been ill for some time and although his passing was mourned by Roman Catholics the world over, his death came as no great surprise. What was surprising, was the short time his successor was to spend as God's representative on earth.

143

Above: Pope John Paul II, former Polish cardinal Karol Wojtyla, after being named as the head of the Catholic Church.

As ever, the conclave of Cardinals met to elect a new Pope, and on this occasion they reached agreement more quickly than usual. White smoke arose from the chimney on 26 August, and the announcement was made that Albino Cardinal Luciani, the Patriarch of Venice, had been elected as the 263rd Pope. Cardinal Luciani in turn announced that he would take John Paul as his Papal name, in honour of his two immediate predecessors.

Pope John Paul I was deemed to be acceptable to both the conservative and liberal wings of the Church and, although he was not in the best of health, he was a mere 65 years old and so his papacy was expected to last for a good while. In the event, it lasted for little more than a month, as he too suffered a heart attack and died on 29 September.

John Paul's successor was Pope John Paul II. Cardinal Wojtyla, the Archbishop of Krakow, Poland, was the first non-Italian Pope to be elected for more than four centuries. In his early years he had attended a seminary in England. John Paul II was just 58 when he became Pope and his reign was to last until 2005. During his papacy he

Below: Firemen at work on a beach in Brittany pumping away crude oil which spilled from the wrecked oil tanker 'Amoco Cadiz'.

travelled to more than 100 countries, and he became the second longest-serving Pope of all time.

Amoco Cadiz disaster

On 18 March 1978, the American owned oil tanker Amoco Cadiz ran aground on Portsall Rocks, off Brittany. It was not the first time a giant tanker had run into trouble, and it would not be the last, but the subsequent oil spillage was the largest of the twentieth century. Storm conditions and a failure in the steering mechanism caused the disaster, and continuing storms and heavy seas hampered an effective clean-up operation over the next two weeks.

The Amoco Cadiz had started out carrying 227,000 tonnes of crude oil from the Gulf, and every tonne ended up in the sea as the ship eventually broke up. The oil slick was 80 miles long and 18 miles wide, and it was to pollute 200 miles of the Brittany coastline. A total of 76 separate Breton communities were affected, and it was 14 years before compensation claims were eventually settled.

Above: Wrecked oil tanker 'Amoco Cadiz' off the coast of Brittany.

1979

FASHION, CULTURE & ENTERTAINMENT

John Wayne dies

Movie Legend John 'Duke' Wayne died of stomach cancer on 11 June 1979. Two days previously he had been baptised into the Roman Catholic Church by the Archbishop of Panama in hospital at the request of his eldest son Michael who gave him a Catholic funeral service.

Born Marion Morrison on 26 May 1907, he was a keen American footballer while at the University of Southern California and began working in local film studios. Actor Tom Mix got him a job in the prop department of William Fox Studios in exchange for

He was 'discovered' by Raoul Walsh who gave him the stage name John Wayne and a starring role in his movie *The Big Trail* in 1930. Despite the commercial

flop of the film, it was the first 'western' epic sound motion picture and established Wayne's reputation. Nine years later, his role in *Stagecoach* made him a star.

Wayne also appeared in more than 20 of Ford's films over 35 years and it is reported that he played the male lead in 142 of his film appearances. He won the Academy Award for Best Actor in *True Grit* in 1969, but

football tickets and Morrison soon started playing bit parts, establishing a friendship with director John Ford.

Above and below: Portraits of John Wayne.

many believe he received it for his contribution to films in a career that spanned more than 40 years.

He was also nominated for Best Actor in *Sands Of Iwo Jima* and as producer of *The Alamo*, one of the two films he directed. His other film, *The Green Berets*, was the only film made in support of the Vietnam War in 1968.

A heavy smoker, Wayne was diagnosed with lung cancer in 1964. He had his entire left lung removed along with two ribs. Famous for his Republican views, Wayne was asked by the Republican Party to run for President in 1968. He declined on the grounds that he did not think the American public would take an actor in the White House seriously! He was married three times and had seven children, four with first wife Josephine Alicia Saenz and three with third wife Pilar Palette.

Ska/2 Tone

Record label 2 Tone was founded by Jerry Dammers, keyboard player with the Specials who, along with Madness, were introducing a music concept to the UK known as ska. 2 Tone had a double meaning: the two tone suits that Jamaican ska musicians usually wore; and, the multi-racial membership of most UK ska bands. The Specials' best known singles include: 'A Message To You Rudy', 'Ghost Town', 'Too Much Too Young' and 'Gangsters'.

Originally a form of Jamaican music, ska began in the early 1960s with traditional mento and calypso elements mixed with American jazz and rhythm and blues. It was the predecessor of reggae and rocksteady and the most listened to music by mods and skinheads.

It gained popularity in the UK during 1979 and the early 1980s and even enjoyed another revival during the 1990s. UK ska artists were respectful to the original Jamaican artists and remade many of the original ska songs – often turning them into hits. Jamaican musician, Prince Buster, made more money from royalties on cover versions than his own records. Despite the cover versions though, 2 Tone recordings definitely had their own sound with faster tempos, full instrumentation and a harder edge.

Ska has had an enormous knock-on effect in the world of music. Bands such as the Clash, the Police and Elvis Costello were all heavily influenced by ska, and the bands that have since been influenced by these and other bands are endless.

The 2 Tone era was named after Dammers' record label and combined Jamaican rhythms of ska with punk rock brutal guitar chords. Lyrics were usually irreverent or politically charged as the 2 Tone genre pushed for racial unity (symbolised by a black and white checker board pattern).

1. TOO MUCH TOO YOUNG*
(Dammers/Chalmers) (2.03)
2. GUNS OF NAVARONE †
(Tiomkin/Webster) (2.25)
THE SPECIALS
Produced by Jerry Dammers & Dave Jordan
*Plangent Visions M. †Chappell M.

CHS TT 7-A

Below: A 2 Tone record.

1979 1978 1977 1976 1975 1974 1973 1972 1971 1970

Sony Walkman

Invented in Japan, the TPS-L2 Walkman that was launched in the UK this year. Despite being expensive at around £100 and somewhat bulky, the Walkman revolutionised the nation. People could walk to work, catch the train or join in the jogging craze while listening to their favourite music.

They became an essential accessory and radio and tape versions were released as well as sport and waterproof ones. They were an instant hit and the first Walkmans had two headphone sockets so friends could share. Inevitably, manufacturers were going to want everyone to own their own and they later got rid of the extra socket.

On 1 July 1999, Sony Corporation celebrated the twentieth anniversary of the Walkman. For more than 25 years, the Walkman has contributed to a new global culture of music enjoyment. The late founder and chief advisor to Sony, Masaru Ibuka and Akio Morita came up with the concept of a portable stereo by taking out the record function and speaker from a cassette tape recorder and equipping it with headphones.

Calvin Klein Jeans

Calvin Klein was instrumental in the birth of designer jeans in 1979. His television adverts and posters were shot by Richard Avedon featuring a skinny, pubescent actress known as Brooke Shields. Born in 1942, Klein taught himself to sketch and sew as a youngster. He won a place at New York's High School of Art and Design and the Fashion Institute of Technology before finally launching his own label with friend and business partner Barry Schwartz in 1968.

As well as pioneering designer jeans, he also raised the profile of underwear and the wholesome all-American look. He has become one of the world's most

Below: The President of Japan's electronics giant Sony, delivers a speech during a press party to commemorate the 25th anniversary of the selling of its first Walkman in 1979.

148

Ed Werner (ex-hockey player turned lawyer). Progress was determined by the players' ability to answer questions on general knowledge or popular culture.

By 1984, more than 20 million games were sold in the US and Canada and the rights were licensed to Parker Brothers, now part of Hasbro, four years later. Richard Branson's Virgin Group had initially turned the game down, but 20 years after its popularity peaked nearly 88 million games had been sold in 26 countries and 17 languages.

Today you can play digital versions of the board game on DVD and online. There are also special editions concentrating on films such as Star Wars and Lord Of The Rings as well as versions aimed specifically at a younger audience.

prolific designers and biggest brand names. Having shaped the casual wear industry, Klein was voted as one of America's most influential people by *Time Magazine*. He has also revolutionised modern advertising, although he is prone to causing a storm over his adverts. He faced controversy over Brooke Shields's jeans advert when she appeared alongside the slogan 'You know what comes between me and my Calvins? Nothing.'

Trivial Pursuit

The board game Trivial Pursuit was developed in 1979 by Scott Abbott (sports editor for the Canadian Press) and Chris Haney (photo editor for the Montreal Gazette) with older brother John (ex-hockey player) and friend

MUSIC

January

Californian schoolgirl Brenda Spencer this month wrote her name in history – and inspired a chart-topping record – when she ran amok with a gun in her San Diego school, shooting two. When questioned afterwards, the teenager was said to have stated that

Above: Another controversial advert from Calvin Klein.
Below: (L-R) Scott Abbott, Chris Haney & John Haney, Canadian inventors of quiz board game Trivial Pursuit, peering from behind a giant reproduction of the game board.

Above: Kate Bush and Bob Geldof.

she did it because 'I don't like Mondays'. The incident and that phrase would ring around the world once more later in the year thanks to Bob Geldof, songwriter and lead singer with the Boomtown Rats (and, in 1985, the force behind Live Aid) who turned it into the title of a UK Number 1 song. He had been doing an interview in

Atlanta, Georgia, when the news came through on the wires, and the single was released less than six months later…fast work by any yardstick.

Despite Spencer's parents' efforts and bans by many radio stations fearing lawsuits, 'Mondays' became the Rats' sole US hit the following March. Geldof still performs it in his solo set – the only song for which he puts down his acoustic guitar and acts out the plot!

April

Following the release of her second album, 'Lionheart', Kate Bush kicked off the only concert tour of her career in Liverpool this month, her show at the city's Empire theatre being the first of 27 dates she would play in just 40 days. The Tour Of Life was as theatrical as Bush's music, and featured dancers, complex lighting and no less than 17 costume changes for the young singer, still three months short of her twenty-first birthday.

It proved to be a financial disaster, but for Bush this paled into insignificance alongside the loss of her lighting director, 21-year-old Bill Duffield, who died after falling 20 feet though an open trap-door at the London

Palladium during her show there on 20 April. She played the penultimate date of the tour, at London's Hammersmith Odeon, as a benefit concert for Duffield's family, and for this was joined by Peter Gabriel and Steve Harley.

Although Bush has never explicitly stated that she won't tour again, it seems the experience was simply too traumatic, and she has since limited her live concert appearances to one-off shows, often for charitable causes.

September

After the disco boom of the early to mid-1970s, and the rise of reggae shortly afterwards, two more black musical styles began to make their presence felt in 1979. As well as ska, spearheaded in the UK by Coventry's 2 Tone label, rap music was making its way from the streets of US cities to the wider world for the first time. Ultimately it would have the wider and longer-lasting impact, as can be seen by its ubiquity in the current millennium.

Rap had been an integral part of 'hip hop' culture, which embraced graffiti, break dancing, and (above all) attitude, for some time, but the Sugarhill Gang's 'Rappers' Delight' marked the point at which rap music finally broke free of its underground origins. Assembled by record executive Sylvia Robinson, the Harlem-based Gang – Michael 'Wonder Mike' Wright, Guy 'Master Gee' O'Brien and Henry 'Big Bank Hank' Jackson – were sued by Chic, whose 'Good Times' backing track they sampled without permission, but their debut hit was the world's first commercially successful rap record.

Above: Kate Bush.

July

Topping the UK charts in July 1979 was a character who could have stepped straight out of a science-fiction film. Gary Numan, 21-year-old white-faced frontman of the electronic group Tubeway Army, was seen on TV screens across the land in pan-stick makeup intoning his highly unusual song 'Are "Friends" Electric'.

Numan, born Gary Webb, had been inspired to follow a pop career by, of all people, the Shadows, and gave up his job at WH Smith to become a pop star with the full backing of his father, who became his manager. His uncle, Jess Lidyard, played drums, keeping Tubeway Army in the family, with Paul Gardiner on bass.

The disc was helped to the top by a limited edition 20,000-pressing picture disc and when the song, a mixture of two Numan compositions, one spoken, one sung, was performed on TV's Top Of The Pops its success was assured. Far from being alienated, his public lapped up the otherworldly performer, whose album 'Replicas' also hit top spot. His career continues today.

December

Disaster struck at the Riverfront Coliseum in Cincinnati this month, when 11 fans died in a crush of people trying to get into the arena for a concert by the Who. Mistaking the band's sound check for the beginning of the concert, fans rushed towards locked entrance doors, and before the doors could be opened many had been crushed or trampled. A subsequent enquiry found that there had been gross crowd management failings, and for over 20 years afterwards the first-come first-

Above: The original line-up of The Who. (L-R) Keith Moon, Pete Townshend, Roger Daltrey and John Entwistle.

served style of seating that had been in use on the night was outlawed in the state of Ohio.

The Who also came in for criticism over the tragedy, with many believing they should have cancelled the evening's gig. But the band were unaware of the events outside the arena, and even if they had known, it's hard to imagine what sort of trouble a decision not to play might have caused.

Some years later, in an interview with *Playboy* magazine, Pete Townshend reflected on how the band had handled the disaster – 'The stampede could have happened at any rock concert. It was much more a symptom of the kids who go to rock-and-roll concerts, being young, getting drunk, doing whatever shitty drugs are available. But that doesn't mean you don't feel guilty, not that it happened but that it was a symbolic moment and we could have handled it right, but we

didn't… I said some dumb things. I said some things that hurt the victims' families. I remember saying, 'It seems that everybody wants us to shed the theatrical tear and to say "sorry". Whereas what we have to do is go on.' The fact is that we didn't have to go on. We could have stopped, and I think we should have stopped. We should have stopped the tour.'

SPORT

First Ryder Cup featuring a European side rather than British Isles

The format of the Ryder Cup changed in 1979 with the Great Britain and Northern Ireland team being expanded to encompass European golfers as well. The competition now comprised four four-ball and four foursome matches on each of the first two days with

Below: The US team line up for a photocall prior to the Ryder Cup at The Greenbrier Club.

1970 1971 1972 1973 1974 1975 1976 1977 1978 1979

12 singles being played on the third for a total of 28 points.

Having a larger pool of players to choose from did not bring victory, however. The Americans won 17-11 at West Virginia's Greenbrier course in White Sulphur Springs to leave their opposition still waiting to claim the cup they had last held in 1957. Nick Faldo registered three wins but was outshone by American Larry Nelson with five.

The inaugural competition was held in 1927, the year after wealthy English merchant Samuel Ryder had watched an impromptu match between British and American golfers who were awaiting the start of the British Open at Royal Lytham & St Annes. After meeting with some competitors it was agreed that he would donate a trophy to be competed for every two years.

The trophy itself was created at a cost of £250 and is a gold chalice 17 inches high, nine inches wide and weighs four pounds. The golfing figure on top was modelled on Ryder's instructor Abe Mitchell who was in line to captain the British team at the first event but who had to pull out because of appendicitis. The first competition was staged by the United States at the Worcester Country Club in Massachusetts and the hosts won by 9.5-2.5.

The US has won the Ryder Cup 24 times since its inception, the British/European team have has registered nine victories and there have been two draws.

It was Jack Nicklaus who proposed the inclusion of European players and this was approved following consultation with Samuel Ryder's descendants to make the competition format what it is today.

Storms wreck Fastnet race

The 1979 Fastnet Race was struck by freak weather conditions in the Irish Sea on 14 August that sank dozens of boats and left 15 people dead. Six died after their safety harnesses snapped while the remainder drowned or perished from hypothermia.

In the biggest peacetime rescue mission, Naval helicopters from RNAS Culdrose in Cornwall joined forces with a Dutch warship and passing ships to help survivors and search for 150 missing yachts in a 20,000 square mile area.

The racers had set off from the Isle of Wight three days earlier on their 600-mile journey across the Irish Sea to round the Fastnet Rock off the coast of Eire and then finish at Plymouth.

Following this race, one of the safety requirements introduced was that all competitors' yachts be equipped with VHF radio after smaller vessels without radios had been unable to report their position.

Below: A Royal Navy helicopter rescues the crew of a yacht after the disastrous Fastnet yacht race.

Trevor Francis becomes UK's first £1 million footballer

Trevor Francis became the UK's most expensive footballer on 9 February 1979 when he moved from Birmingham City to Nottingham Forest for a record £1,000,000. The magical seven-figure transfer fee doubled the previous record of £500,000 West

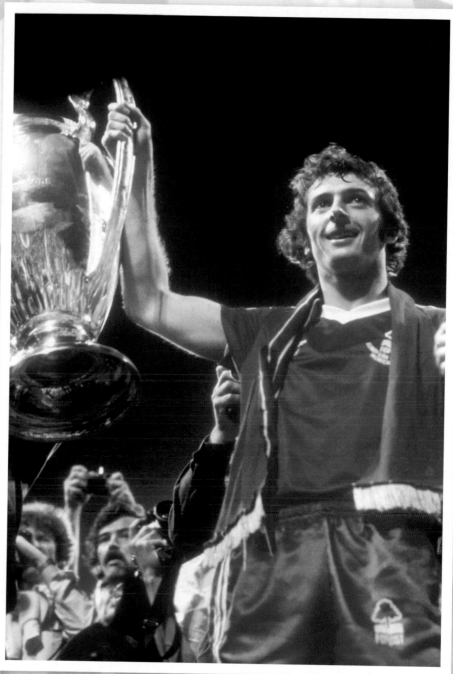

Bromwich Albion paid to Middlesbrough for the services of David Mills just three months earlier.

Trevor John Francis, born 19 April 1954 in Plymouth, had broken into the Birmingham City team as a 16-year-old and he immediately set about repaying the record fee. Forest claimed the League Cup – Francis was ineligible for the Final – were going well in the League and had won through to the semi-final of the European Cup against FC Cologne.

Above: Trevor Francis of Nottingham Forest celebrates scoring the winning goal by lifting the cup after the European Cup Final between Nottingham Forest and Malmo, May, 1979.

They overcame the Germans by an aggregate 4-3 scoreline to book their place in the Final in Munich against Swedish side Malmo but faltered in the League to eventually finish eight points behind Champions Liverpool (ironically their First Round opponents in that season's European Cup!).

Francis, making his European debut for Forest at the expense of Martin O'Neill, scored the only goal of the showpiece Final when he headed home John Robertson's cross just before half-time. This sent Nottingham delirious and manager Brian Clough took the famous trophy back to the City Ground where it stayed for two years after they successfully defended their title against Hamburg the following year.

Failing to fulfil his potential at Forest, Francis was sold to Manchester City in 1981 and later played for Sampdoria, Atalanta, Glasgow Rangers, QPR and Sheffield Wednesday before retiring in 1994. Francis has tried his hand at management with numerous clubs and is a regular TV commentator.

The current British transfer record is the £29.1 million paid by Manchester United to Leeds United for Rio Ferdinand in July 2002 while the world record is held by Real Madrid when they bought Zinedine Zidane from Juventus for £46 million.

POLITICS & CURRENT AFFAIRS

Winter of discontent

When William Shakespeare penned Richard III and wrote the 'now is the winter of our discontent' speech, he probably didn't realize that, several hundred years later, one Larry Lamb, the editor of *The Sun*, would misquote him. It was however Mr Lamb who first used the term 'winter of discontent' in an editorial for his August journal. Almost 30 years later, most people who were alive during 1978/79 recognise the meaning of it.

The late 1970s was proving to be a very difficult period for almost everyone in Britain. At times the very fabric of society seemed to be threatened, with unrest, militancy and general discord abundant. Perhaps Harold Wilson had known what he was doing when he handed over to James Callaghan in 1976 as, within a couple of years, it really did seem that the country was becoming ungovernable.

Above: A woman walks past a pavement piled high with rubbish due to a refuse collector's strike during the 'Winter of Discontent'.

private and public sectors, were submitting wage demands far in excess of 5%, per cent, and soon the mounting industrial unrest manifested itself in strike action. Lorry drivers were amongst the first to strike and, during January and February 1979, other groups joined in. It was not long before local council workers took industrial action, and the rubbish began to pile up – first in the streets and then on commons and other open spaces. It is the heaps of rubbish and consequent health hazards which people remember – as well as a strike by gravediggers which resulted in bodies being piled up in mortuaries.

The winter of discontent signalled the end for Callaghan's Labour government. A certain Margaret Thatcher was waiting to pounce.

Thatcher triumphant

On 4 May 1979, Margaret Thatcher became Britain's first woman prime minister. The country had turned to the Conservatives in the wake of the 'Winter of Discontent' and now

Britain's loan from the International Monetary Fund meant that the government had been forced to cut public spending. An attempt was made to limit pay rises to 5%, but in July 1978 the TUC rejected this 'voluntary' policy out of hand. Many groups of workers, in both the

Below: Labour politician and prime minister, James Callaghan, at a political conference.

1970 1971 1972 1973 1974 1975 1976 1977 1978 1979

1970 1971 1972 1973 1974 1975 1976 1977 1978 1979

the Iron Lady, as she would soon come to be called, stood on the doorstep of number 10 Downing Street – and prepared to do battle with the unions, and with anyone else who stood in her way. On that doorstep she quoted St Francis of Assisi, and famously said:

'Where there is discord, may we bring harmony. Where there is error, may we bring truth. Where there is doubt, may we bring faith. And where there is despair, may we bring hope.'

It was not clear whether Mrs Thatcher was using the Royal 'We', or whether she was involving husband Dennis in her predictions.

The Conservatives had won 339 seats to Labour's 269, and they had an overall majority of 43 in the new parliament – more than enough to govern effectively. From the beginning of her reign, it was clear that Margaret Thatcher was to be no pushover. Jeremy Thorpe, the former leader of the Liberal Party who was now awaiting trial for conspiracy and incitement to murder, commented that she made Edward Heath look like a moderate. Some felt she made Genghis Khan look like a moderate.

The Thatcher years were to transform Britain. During the election campaign the new prime minister had said the Conservatives would cut taxes, reduce public expenditure, make it easier for people to buy their own homes, and curb the power of the unions. They did all of these things, but the transformation was far from painless for many UK citizens. The Iron Lady ruled until 1990, when she was

Above and below: Margaret Thatcher.

dispatched by her own party in what might perhaps be called a bloodless coup. She was very upset.

Blunt exposed

Sir Anthony Blunt was very much an establishment figure. A brilliant art historian, he had held many important posts in the art world, and had been knighted for his services in 1956. He came from an aristocratic background and, being distantly related to the Queen, he became the keeper of the royal family's drawings and pictures.

Blunt, however, had a secret. And it was a big one. As a student, he had been recruited by the KGB as early as 1934, and had passed secrets to the Soviet Union from then, until after the Second World War. MI5 were told about Blunt's spying activities in 1963, but he was not publicly exposed until 1979, when it was revealed that he had been a part of the Cambridge University spy ring, which included Kim Philby, Guy Burgess and Donald Maclean. The Queen was not amused. Blunt was stripped of his knighthood, and he died in disgrace in 1983.

Above: Sir Anthony Blunt, British art historian and Surveyor of the Queen's Pictures.

Images Supplied Courtesy of:

GETTY IMAGES
101 Bayham Street, London NW10AG

Concept and Art Direction:
Vanessa and Kevin Gardner

Design & Artwork:
Jane Stephens

Publishers:
Vanessa Gardner & Jules Gammond

Edited by:
Michael Heatley

Written by:
Alan Kinsman, Chris Mason, Ian Welch and Claire Welch

51965